MICHIGAN-ONTARIO
IRON ORE RAILROADS

MICHIGAN-ONTARIO IRON ORE RAILROADS

PATRICK C. DORIN

TLC
PUBLISHING INC.

© Copyright 2002 TLC Publishing, Inc.

1387 Winding Creek Lane
Lynchburg, VA 24503-3776

International Standard Book Number   1-883089-72-7
Library of Congress Control Number   2002101139

Design and Production by
Kevin J. Holland
type&DESIGN
Burlington, Ontario

Produced on the MacOS™

Printed by
Walsworth Publishing Company
Marceline, Missouri 64658

Front cover—
Three Milwaukee Road F-units led by FP7A No. 63A head up an ore train at Antoine, Michigan, on October 28, 1978.
The yard is near Iron Mountain, where the Milwaukee Road and Chicago & North Western exchanged empty and loaded
ore trains for the Groveland Mine during the last few years of the Menominee Range ore pool. STEVE GLISCHINSKI

Title page—
An Algoma Central Railway (Wisconsin Central) ore train at Michipicoten in February 1995. STEVE GLISCHINSKI

Other books by Patrick C. Dorin from TLC Publishing, Inc.—

Western Pacific Locomotives and Equipment
Louisville & Nashville—The Old Reliable (with Charles Castner and Ron Flanary)
Louisville & Nashville Passenger Trains—The Pan American Era 1921–1971 (with Charles Castner and Robert Chapman)
Chicago & North Western Passenger Service—The Postwar Years
Chicago & North Western Passenger Equipment
The Challenger
Missouri Pacific Freight Trains and Equipment
Missouri Pacific Passenger Service—The Postwar Years
Minnesota–Ontario Iron Ore Railroads

Dedicated to the memory of

Clayton McFaul

Career-long employee of the Soo Line Railroad and Wisconsin Central Railway
who shared his thorough knowledge of the
Gogebic Iron Range operations.

ACKNOWLEDGMENTS

Although I have written it many times, no book would ever be possible without the assistance and wisdom of many people. I would like to thank the generous individuals who provided photographs, advice, proofreading, and additional research for this book.

John Marshal, Susan Malette, Michael Silta, and many others on the Lake Superior & Ishpeming Railroad reviewed the text and provided information on LS&I ore car equipment and train operations.

John Belsky, Arlene Mews, Steve Beronek, and Kelly Ross provided assistance on the Wisconsin Central, the Sault Ste. Marie Bridge Company, and the Algoma Central.

Additional information came from John Bergene for the Soo Line Railroad, Andy Roth of the Soo Line Technical and Historical Society, Joseph Piersen of the C&NW Historical Society, Tim Schandel of the Lake Superior Railroad Museum, and Northern Illinois University.

Kevin Acker provided some of the maps, and Robert Blomquist assisted with research on ore car equipment rosters and photographs.

Thanks also to Fred Headon, Dale Wilson, and Gordon Jomini for photographs and information regarding the Canadian National and Canadian Pacific ore operations in the Province of Ontario.

Steve Glischinski shared photographs and information on the Escanaba & Lake Superior Railroad and the Milwaukee Road.

The following people provided an incredible number of invaluable photographs to enhance the chapters: Robert C. Anderson, Michael Burlaga, Thomas Dorin, Gordon DeHaas, Ken Johnson, J. Michael Gruber, Owen Leander, Dan Mackey, Joel Nagro, Al Paterson, Joe Piersen, Kent Rengo, David C. Schauer, and Harold K. Vollrath.

My wife Karen spent many hours proofreading and on the road assisting with research and photography work. Thomas W. Dixon, Jr. of TLC Publishing encouraged this two-volume project, and Kevin J. Holland performed the book's design and layout work.

To all, a huge "thank you" in a thousand different ways. Should an acknowledgment have inadvertently been missed in this section, please accept my apology and trust it will be in the appropriate place within the text. Again a SOO-per *thank you*.

INTRODUCTION

Michigan-Ontario Iron Ore Railroads covers the wide variety of ore-hauling railroads in northern Wisconsin, Upper Michigan, and Ontario, primarily since the 1970s with some backtracking into the 1950s and 1960s for ore operations that disappeared during the mid-century. These railroad lines handled ore from the Gogebic, Menominee, and Marquette Ranges through the ports of Ashland and Marquette on Lake Superior; and Escanaba on Lake Michigan. Still other iron ore mining operations in Ontario sent ore through Little Current and Depot Harbor on Lake Huron, and Michipicoten on Lake Superior.

Several railroads, such as the Chicago & North Western, the Milwaukee Road, and the Duluth, South Shore & Atlantic, have either been folded into mergers, or are out of the ore business. The Canadian National and Canadian Pacific operations on Lake Huron have ceased, as has the Algoma Central operation serving Lake Superior.

On the other hand, the Wisconsin Central took over the ore operations of the Chicago & North Western lines when the Union Pacific decided to withdraw from Upper Michigan. Furthermore, the Wisconsin Central has become extensively involved in all-rail movements as well as handling Minnesota taconite pellets to Escanaba. The Canadian National is now back in the ore business with its acquisition of the Wisconsin Central. Meanwhile, the Lake Superior & Ishpeming Railroad continues to serve the Marquette Range with its railroad and ore dock system.

The companion volume to this book, *Minnesota-Ontario Iron Ore Railroads*, describes the ore operations in northeastern Minnesota and northwestern Ontario.

Hopefully readers will find both books useful not only for historical purposes and providing an understanding of ore-handling logistics, but as an aid to modeling these diverse and colorful railroad systems.

Patrick C. Dorin
Superior, Wisconsin
July 15, 2002

CONTENTS

When Canadian National purchased the Wisconsin Central it acquired the WC's Michigan ore lines and the Minorca trains between the DM&IR connection at Steelton (Duluth) to Escanaba. This January 2002 train is a Minorca empty at Prentice, Wisconsin. KENT RENGO

1

THE LAKE SUPERIOR &

ABOVE: Although the LS&I was (and is) primarily an ore hauler, the company once provided freight service throughout its system from Republic east to Munising. The company served the paper mill at Munising. In this case, the local freight has departed Munising and is westbound at Munising Junction en route to Marquette in July 1972. GORDON DEHAAS

FACING PAGE: During the 1990s, General Electric U-Boats became the standard power on the LS&I. Most came from the Burlington Northern still wearing the Cascade Green color scheme. It is a beautiful summer day in July 1995, and the brakes are hot as the train approaches the Marquette ore yard. DAVID C. SCHAUER

The Lake Superior & Ishpeming has served the Marquette Iron Range since the railroad's beginning in 1896, and it continues to function at the turn of the 21st century as a very effective ore hauler.

LS&I trains continue to operate between the port of Marquette, the Eagle Mills operating center, and the mining area. From Eagle Mills, the mine run assignments currently (2002) serve the Tilden and Empire mines plus the Republic mine for special ore orders at the far western end of the railroad.

This chapter describes LS&I train operations since the 1970s, as well as the railroad's motive power and its ore car fleet, one of the most diverse in North America.

The LS&I operations can be divided into four groups, almost all of which are

ISHPEMING RAILROAD

LS&I No. 2301 leads a mixture of freight cars and ore cars at Negaunee, Michigan. Part of this section of the LS&I was once a joint operating venture for the LS&I, the Soo Line (Ex-DSS&A territory) and the Chicago & North Western. Signals to the right mark this as CTC territory. GORDON DeHAAS

What typifies the LS&I ore train operations as they roll into the 21st century? Green ex-Burlington Northern General Electrics for power with a wide mixture of rebuilt ore cars originally purchased by the LS&I as well as modified and rebuilt ore cars from the DM&IR and the Canadian National. The sun is setting as it shines on an eastbound 60-car loaded ore train en route from the Tilden Mine to Eagle Mills in August 1996. PATRICK C. DORIN

There is incredible scenery and rock cuts from Marquette toward Eagle Mills and beyond to the mining area. The photographer caught the dramatic combination of the beauty of nature and an LS&I ore train at Eagle Mills Junction on July 7, 1995. DAVID C. SCHAUER

controlled out of the "Operating Center" at Eagle Mills. Besides the abandonment of the lines east of Marquette and the connections with the Manistique & Lake Superior Railroad for the "Ford" ore, the real difference in LS&I train operations since the 1970s is the service to and from the ore dock in Marquette.

Ore dock train services are handled by two assignments. One set of operations goes down the hill from Eagle Mills. The crews normally make two round trips depending upon the extent of switching required at Eagle Mills. As of 1996, two General Electric units were assigned to these particular train operations. During the 1970s and 1980s, it was not uncommon for this assignment to have a mixture of up to three Alco and GE units. This operation is known as the Hill Job.

Another assignment originates in Marquette and is known as the Dock-Hill. The crew moves loaded cars of pellets from the ore yard to the ore dock, as well as making a trip up the hill to the Eagle Mills yards. The Marquette ore dock operations are also assigned two General Electrics.

A Dock Job simply works at the ore dock, but may have other assignments.

All assignments are based on shiploading schedules with a usual minimum of four round trips between the Marquette ore dock and yard and Eagle Mills every 24 hours. However, the number can expand to as many as six or eight round trips depending upon ship loading requirements. The entire railroad is classified as "Yard Limits."

It is interesting to note that the Lake Superior & Ishpeming's ore trains during the 1960s operated between Marquette and Eagle Mills as well as all the way to Harris Yard in Negaunee. The trains out of Marquette were assigned cabooses, but the mine run operations were not equipped with cabooses.

As of the late 1990s, other train operations out of Eagle Mills included the assignments to Tilden, Empire, Ishpeming, and Republic. Depending upon boat loading schedules and mining company needs, there may be two or three such assignments during the day, afternoon, and midnight shifts.

The Eagle Mills assignments also handled all of the Chicago & North Western (subsequently Union Pacific and later, Wisconsin Central) switching and placement of ore cars loading at the Tilden. The WC, actually the Sault Ste. Marie Bridge Company (SSAM), delivers empties for the Tilden Mine at Eagle Mills.

The LS&I delivers the loads back to the SSAM at Partridge. (The WC delivers empties and picks up loads at the Empire Mine.)

One of the interesting facets about the ore operations on the LS&I is the flexibility to meet mining company and other shipper needs. For example, a Marquette dock crew may dump pellets on the ore dock for part of the assignment, and then make up a train and run directly to Eagle Mills. It is this type of flexibility that creates "effective" service levels for the two mines shipping pellets and special orders for the Republic mine.

ABOVE: A view of the LS&I roundhouse and the east end of Ishpeming, Michigan, on July 6, 1956.

BELOW LEFT: Lake Superior & Ishpeming Alco RS-3 No. 1604, built in September 1950, switches at Munising, Michigan, on June 30, 1956.

BELOW RIGHT: LS&I combine No. 12, a product of the Ohio Falls Car Co. of Jeffersonville, Indiana, resided at Munising on June 30, 1956. ALL, TLC PUBLISHING COLLECTION

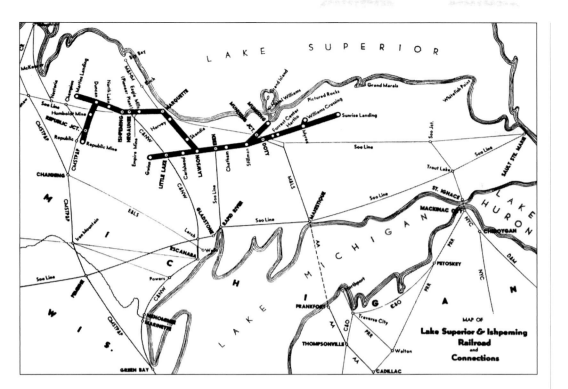

MAPPING THE LS&I

The LS&I has a very high traffic density for a railroad of its size. It serves an absolutely beautiful area of the Upper Peninsula of Michigan, and the ore trains would make for a profound model railroad system.

The accompanying map illustrates the extent of the LS&I during the 1960s. Note the Manistique & Lake Superior Railroad line from Manistique to Doty, Michigan—the connection for the all-rail shipments of Ford ore.

In 2002, all lines east of Marquette have been abandoned with the exception of the Munising-to-Munising Junction segment, which

is now owned and operated by the Wisconsin Central (CN).

A branch segment extends from Eagle Mills to the Tilden and Empire Mines with connec-

A loaded train behind ex-BN U-Boats passes a "Dock-Hill" job and arrives at the departure yard for the Marquette dock in August 1995. PATRICK C. DORIN

The "Dock-Hill" job is lined up for departure. PATRICK C. DORIN

A train has been loaded at the Tilden Mine and is about to depart for Eagle Mills in August 1995. Two U30Cs are the normal power assignments for the mine runs.

Looking back at the loads of the Tilden ore run, note how the iron ore pellets fill the cars to the top of the extensions.

The loading facility at the Tilden Mine. ALL, PATRICK C. DORIN

The loading facility at the Empire Mine in August 1995.

East of Eagle Mills, there is an automatic scale on the main line for weighing the ore trains enroute to the Marquette dock. The track at left in the photo is the former Duluth, South Shore & Atlantic Railroad main line toward Marquette. This view was recorded in August 1995.

tions with the Sault Ste. Marie Bridge Company (Wisconsin Central) at Eagle Mills and Partridge Junction just south of Eagle Mills.

The line still extends from Eagle Mills to Duncan and the Republic Mine on the far west end of the LS&I.

Total LS&I mileage had contracted from 130 miles in 1969 to only 49 miles in 2002.

FREIGHT TRAIN OPERATIONS

Although the LS&I has not served the paper mill at Munising, Michigan, since 1989 (The WC now owns the trackage to the Kimberly Clark mill.), the railroad still handles commercial freight. Most of the traffic includes clay, lime-stone, and caustic soda for the pelletizing plants. The LS&I once operated an extensive freight service over the routes that have been abandoned since the 1960s.

Part of the LS&I's freight traffic consists of covered hopper cars loaded with Bentonite clay for the pelletizing process at the Tilden and Empire plants. Although it is August 1995, this car still proudly carried its Burlington Route insignia—25 years after the Burlington Northern merger. ALL, PATRICK C. DORIN

FACING PAGE, TOP: The 3:00 pm Marquette ore dock assignment has just completed assembling a shove for the dock on August 24, 1996. The ore dock yard office is located to the left of No. 3011. The Marquette ore yard is unique in that dock movements ("shoves") must pull out of the yard before moving onto the ore dock approach.

FACING PAGE, BOTTOM: The six-track Marquette ore yard is visible alongside the ore dock approach.

The shove is making progress as it curves around the approach toward the dock.

Arrival of a shove on top of the LS&I's Marquette dock. Note that there is little space between the dock tracks—this is the reason Michigan ore cars are narrower than their Minnesota counterparts.

The ex-DM&IR ore cars just ahead of the locomotive have been rebuilt and made a bit narrower so that they will fit on the ore dock.
ALL, PATRICK C. DORIN

TOP: This 1996 view of the Marquette ore dock shows the power plant coal receiving facility adjacent to the LS&I yard and dock approach. Ships handle Wyoming coal from Superior, Wisconsin, to Marquette for the power company.

The LS&I ore dock prior to construction of the coal receiving bin.

The road to Presque Isle Park on the far north side of Marquette goes under the ore dock.

Ex-Santa Fe 2400-horsepower Alco "Alligator" road switchers also handled ore dock shoves in years past. ALL, PATRICK C. DORIN

THE LS&I ORE CAR FLEET

The Lake Superior & Ishpeming Railroad ore car fleet has remained substantially the same since the 1960s, with some rather interesting additions. Except for the jumbo red-and-black ore cars of 85-ton capacity, all of the LS&I ore cars have been rebuilt with extensions to accommodate pellet traffic.

The LS&I has the most varied ore car fleet to be found in the Lake Superior region. It is the only railroad in the Lake Superior region still operating ore cars with comparatively small 55-ton capacities.

On the other hand, the company is also operating a fleet of ex-Duluth, Missabe & Iron Range ore cars in two different configurations. The first group consists of cars without extensions or any modifications. (Modelers know these as a perfect match for the Walthers HO-scale ore car model.) The second group has been extensively rebuilt with side extensions, and the width of the cars has been reduced for close-clearance operation on the ore dock. The DM&IR ore cars, as is, are too wide for the trackage on the LS&I dock and cannot be placed side by side on adjacent tracks. Thus the cars were rebuilt with yellow-painted side extensions, reduced width, and are known as "Banana Tops" (although later paint jobs did not include the yellow tops).

With the exception of the red jumbo ore cars, a number of ex-DM&IR ore cars, and the newest additions to the ore car fleet from the Long Island Railroad in 2001, the entire Lake Superior & Ishpeming fleet is painted black with white lettering.

Modelers will note that the LS&I ore car series 7000 to 7149 is virtually identical to the HO-scale Model Die Casting tapered-side car.

This spectacular view of the LS&I ore dock was taken in May 1952. Two LS&I Alco RS-1s are spotting loaded ore cars on the dock—quite a contrast with the ex-BN U30Cs and extended-side cars of more recent years. The *International* is loading, while another ship is "smoking it up" on the opposite side. ELMER TRELOAR, PATRICK C. DORIN COLLECTION

The 1000-footer *Great Lakes Trader* loads on the south side of the LS&I's Marquette dock on June 27, 2001, while another vessel loads on the north side. In 2002, the LS&I dock marked 90 years of operation providing a very effective rail-to-water service. PATRICK C. DORIN

GREAT LAKES TRADER

SUMMARY OF ORE CARS 1980–2001

All 50-ton ore cars numbered 1 to 1040, and 1100 to 1399 were scrapped.

50-Ton Ore Cars

1400-1499	83 cars
1500-1599	84 cars
1600-1699	87 cars
1700-1799	90 cars
1800-1899	83 cars
Total	427 cars as of February 1997

70-Ton Ore Cars

7000-7199	192 cars in mid-1980s (Tapered-side cars)
7200-7899	622 cars in mid-1980s
7000-7899	113 cars in mid-1990s

85-Ton Ore Cars

8000-8199	184 cars in mid-1980s
	160 cars in 1997

89-Ton Ore Cars

8500-8599	78 cars in mid-1980s
	51 cars in 1997

Ex-DM&IR 77-Ton Ore Cars

9000-9099	91 cars in mid-1980s
	87 cars in 1997
9100-9199	91 cars in mid-1980s
	83 cars in 1997
9200-9299	95 cars in mid-1980s
	92 cars in 1997
9300-9399	98 cars in mid-1980s
	90 cars in 1997
9400-9499	100 cars in mid-1980s
	98 cars in 1997
9600-9659	58 cars in mid-1980s
9600-9699	94 cars in 1997

Ex-Canadian National / Long Island Railroad / Burlington Northern / Northern Pacific 77-Ton or 82-Ton capacity ore cars rebuilt in 2001

9500-9599	100 cars purchased from the Long Island, which acquired the cars from CN and BN.

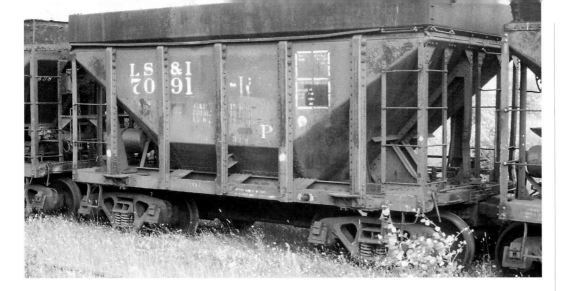

FACING PAGE, TOP: LS&I ore car No. 1508, at Marquette in August 1995, was part of the last group of the 50-ton capacity ore cars in operation. PATRICK C. DORIN

FACING PAGE, MIDDLE: No. 1577 is another example of a rebuilt 50-ton car. The load limit when photographed in 1995 was listed as 135,700 pounds, or 67.8 tons. PATRICK C. DORIN

FACING PAGE, BOTTOM: Rebuilt ore car No. 1844 with its lettering and numbers nice and bright. The 1800s were the top end of the group of 50-ton-plus capacity cars still in operation in the late 1990s. PATRICK C. DORIN

No. 7091, at Harris Yard in August 1995 and part of the 7000-7149 series, is virtually identical to the Model Die Casting tapered-side HO-scale ore car. PATRICK C. DORIN

The remainder of the 7000 series cars, such as 7638 at Harris Yard in August 1995, did not have the same type of lip at the top of the main section of the tapered side. Note the differences between the 7638 and the 7091, just below the extension. Some of this equipment has been sold to the Wisconsin Central and in 2001 was being relettered for WC subsidiary Sault Ste. Marie Bridge Company (SSAM). PATRICK C. DORIN

Ore car No. 8078, at Marquette in August 1995, was part of the last group of ore cars ordered by the LS&I. They were built by Bethlehem Steel Company in 1965. The cars have a capacity of 170,000 pounds or 85 tons. PATRICK C. DORIN

Car No. 8565 was part of a 1964 order from Bethlehem Steel. Known as "Huskies," they were the only LS&I ore cars painted red.

Car No. 8080, at Marquette in August 1996, has been rebuilt and was one of three such ore cars to carry an LS&I insignia celebrating a century of service.

Car No. 9111, at Marquette in August 1995, is part of an ex-DM&IR group rebuilt for service on the LS&I ore dock. Yellow extensions earned the cars the nickname "Banana Tops."

LS&I No. 8068, at Eagle Mills on August 4, 1998, was one of several cars modified with air-operated doors.

No. 25612 is an ex-DM&IR car, photographed in 1995.
ALL, PATRICK C. DORIN

"Banana Top" No. 9378 shows its yellow-painted extension at Marquette in August 1995. PATRICK C. DORIN

One more example of a rebuilt ex-DM&IR car, No. 9226, in service on the LS&I at Marquette in August 1995. PATRICK C. DORIN

The LS&I owned and operated a fleet of off-set side hoppers for coal service. Cars 5215, 5162, and 5198 are shown here at the Marquette coal dock on a bright sunny day in May 1975. GORDON DE HAAS

The company owns two covered hoppers for sand service. Numbered 1 and 2, the cars were photographed at the Eagle Mills locomotive facility in August 1996. PATRICK C. DORIN

LS&I gondola 6757, at Eagle Mills in August 1996, has been modified for maintenance-of-way work. The car once served in a variety of functions including pulpwood service. Note the placement of the insignia in the center of the car. PATRICK C. DORIN

The jumbo coal hopper fleet was purchased for coal service to the mines and power plants as needed, especially for emergency services. PATRICK C. DORIN

The LS&I, although primarily an ore hauler, did operate a number of box cars for paper and other traffic. PS-1 car No. 2503, at Eagle Mills in August 1998, shows the typical lettering seen during the 1980s and 1990s. PATRICK C. DORIN

Flat car No. 6401, photographed at Eagle Mills in August 1998, is a low bulkhead design for a variety of services on the Marquette Range. PATRICK C. DORIN

All-door box car No. 2018 is an example of the modern box cars on the LS&I. PATRICK C. DORIN

LS&I Scale Test Car No. 5 is painted a bright jade green.

No. 9528, at Eagle Mills on June 27, 2001, is the newest variation in the LS&I ore car fleet. The company purchased 100 cars from the Long Island Railroad, which were actually operated by the New York & Atlantic Railroad for handling pulverized granite to an asphalt plant. However, part of the new fleet are former Canadian National ore cars. Note the four braces. The cars are painted in a slightly lighter shade of box car red with white lettering. No. 9431 to the left is a former DM&IR car. The new fleet is being numbered in the 9500 series.

LS&I 9525 illustrates the "B" end of the ex-LI and CN cars. Note how Canadian National placed the hand brake and end platform at a higher level in line with the extension.

The former LI/CN ore cars are being rebuilt by the LS&I, with the width being reduced by 8 inches (4 inches on each side) to permit operation on the ore dock. The extreme width of the ex-CN cars was 10 feet, 8 inches. The new width compares favorably with the LS&I's largest ore cars, the 8500 to 8599-series "Huskies," which were 10 feet, 2 inches wide. Long Island 4091 is shown here stored at Eagle Mills on June 27, 2001, awaiting rebuilding. ALL, PATRICK C. DORIN

LS&I steel caboose No. 2 was painted in a jade green scheme with yellow striping and the modern LS&I insignia when photographed at Eagle Mills in August 1984.
THOMAS A. DORIN

No. 1606 was part of a small fleet of RS-3s on the LS&I, Nos. 1604 to 1611. The original colors were a very attractive red and yellow. No. 1606 was switching the freight house at Marquette in 1957.
GORDON DEHAAS

RS-3 No. 1609 was repainted maroon with gold lettering. The Alco was photographed at the Marquette roundhouse in the 1970s.
PATRICK C. DORIN

MOTIVE POWER

The LS&I motive power roster has completely changed over from a fleet of Alcos in the 1960s, purchased from Alco and the Santa Fe, to a group of General Electric U30Cs in the 1990s—again in this case, both a group of its own purchased from GE, and a secondhand fleet from Burlington Northern. Color schemes have ranged from a solid dark red and a solid yellow to rather spectacular greens with orange and white lettering, and reds with the same insignias. The predominant color in the 1990s was BN green with LS&I lettering. LS&I motive power operates primarily in ore and freight train service for the company, but its power is often leased to Wisconsin Central during the time the Marquette dock is shut down from January through March. The WC often uses the leased power to handle ore between the Mesabi Range and Escanaba, as well as all-rail ore moves from the Tilden Mine to Algoma Steel in Sault Ste. Marie, Ontario.

LS&I MOTIVE POWER ROSTER SUMMARY

Type	Series	Remarks
RS-1	1001 - 1003	Built in 1951 and retired by 1967.
RS-2	1501 - 1503	Built in 1949 and retired in 1969.
RS-3	1604 - 1611	Built 1950 to 1955, and all retired between 1965 and 1989. With the exception of the 1611, all were delivered in the red scheme with yellow stripe. Majority were later painted in the solid maroon scheme.
RSD-12	1801 - 1804	Built 1956 to 1963. Painted red with yellow stripe when delivered. Painted maroon after 1968. The 1801 was rebuilt with a chop nose and 2000 h.p. and painted yellow in 1964. Nos. 1802 and 1804 were repainted in green scheme.
RSD-12	1850 - 1853	Purchased in 1972 from the B&O, lettered LASCO and numbered 2007 - 2010. Later renumbered 1800 and 1805 - 1807. Third set of numbers were in the 1850s. While numbered 1800, 1805 - 1807 the units were painted maroon. When renumbered to the 1850s, the units were green.
RSD-12	2014, 2016	Purchased from General Electric (ex-B&O) by LASCO in 1972, but sold to the Utah Railway by 1974.
RSD-15	2400-2405	Purchased from the Santa Fe in 1975 and painted maroon. As of 1983, the units were painted in red scheme with the exception of the 2403. All sold to the Green Bay & Western in 1989.
U25C	2500 - 2501	Built in 1964 with the yellow scheme. Repainted maroon in 1968 - 1969. The 2501 was repainted in the red scheme in 1986. Both retired in 1989.
U23C	2300 - 2304	Built from 1968 to late 1970. All units delivered in the maroon paint scheme. The 2300 was repainted in the green scheme. The 2301 was repainted red.
U30C	3000 - 3008	Built in 1974 for the Burlington Northern.
	3009 - 3011	Built in 1975 for the BN (No. 3011 built in 1974).
	3013	
	3050 - 3053	Built in 1974 for the BN.

LS&I Motive Power—2001

Type	Series			
U30C	3000		C-30-7	3071 - 3074
	3003 - 3006			
	3008 - 3011			
	3051 - 3053			

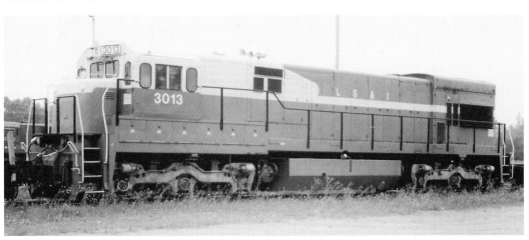

RSD-12s 1800-1804 were the first C-C (six-wheel trucks) units on the LS&I. Originally painted red with yellow stripes, No. 1800 is shown in solid maroon at Marquette in May 1975. GORDON DE HAAS

RSD-12 Nos. 1802 and 1851 illustrate the green LS&I scheme at Eagle Mills in August 1984. Thomas A. Dorin

LS&I 2402, at Eagle Mills in September 1984, was one of six RSD-15s owned by the company. Paint was a bright red with yellow striping and two white stripes on the end. THOMAS A. DORIN

The LS&I purchased two U25C's in a yellow scheme from General Electric in 1964. No. 2500 was at Marquette on July 2, 1973. ROBERT C. ANDERSON

A General Electric in Detroit Edison's blue and silver colors was lettered LS&I and given the number 3013. PATRICK C. DORIN

ABOVE: In the 1990s, the most modern power operated by the C&NW was the SD60, like No. 8026 leading a loaded ore train from the Marquette Range to Escanaba, and photographed at Goose Lake on July 7, 1995. DAVID C. SCHAUER

FACING PAGE: During the loading process at C&NW's low-level ore dock at Escanaba, Michigan, ore pellets were transported to the traveling ship loader via a conveyor belt as shown here with the loading of the lake boat *Henry Ford II*. C&NW PHOTO, PATRICK C. DORIN COLLECTION

It could be said that this chapter belongs to an "out of the business" section, but the operations have continued without a blink of an eye from the C&NW to the UP to the Wisconsin Central (the latter being the subject of the next chapter).

Massive changes have taken place with the Chicago & North Western's ore hauling since the 1960s. The year 1967 saw the closing of the Peterson Mine on the Gogebic Iron Range, which in turn put an end to all of the ore operations between the Ironwood, Michigan, area and Escanaba. The Groveland Mine near Randville on the Milwaukee Road (and later the Escanaba & Lake Superior Railroad) closed in 1982, putting an end to the mining operations on the Menominee Range. Consequently the C&NW, which merged with the Union Pacific, served only

WESTERN/UNION PACIFIC

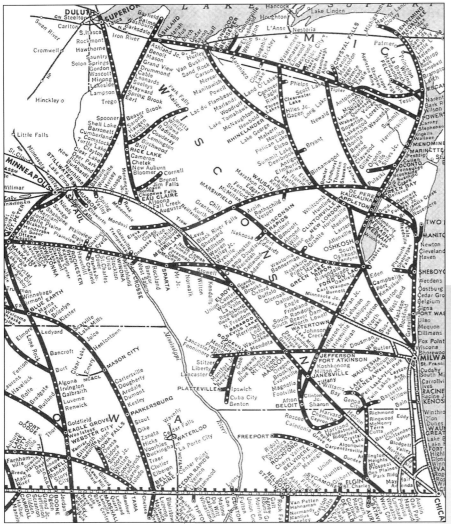

the Marquette Range with its line from Escanaba to Ishpeming.

The C&NW ore car fleet in 1960 operated as built. By the mid-1970s, the fleet was being reduced in size but made more round trips with ore than ever. Most of the fleet had been fitted with 18-inch side extensions for greater cubic capacity of iron ore pellets, which are less dense than the natural, unprocessed ore.

Still other major changes began in 1968 when wooden dock No. 6 in Escanaba was dismantled and replaced with a low-level, conveyor-type facility equipped with a traveling ship loader. This changed the entire configuration of the Escanaba ore terminal.

The loaded ore cars are dumped by a rotary dumper, with the pellets moving on conveyor

C&NW ore lines extended from Duluth to Escanaba. Primary ore routes since the 1940s extended from the Ironwood, Michigan, area to both Ashland and Escanaba, and from Ishpeming to Escanaba. Gogebic ore moved from Ironwood to Duluth via Ashland, Spooner, and Superior. All-rail routes extended south from Ishpeming, Hurley, and Superior. South of Superior, loaded trains operated via Spooner and Hudson, Wis., before heading to Chicago. All-rail routes in 2002 included UP trackage rights over BNSF and WC south of Superior. C&NW

An eastbound 46-car ore train moves through Florence, Wisconsin, en route to Escanaba behind Milwaukee Road 2-8-2 No. 330 on July 31, 1948. The ore is from the Iron River area, and more cars will be added at Iron Mountain.
AL PATERSON COLLECTION

belts to a stacker for the stock piles. With the arrival of a boat, the pellets are transported by conveyor belt to the dock system and loaded directly into the vessel. The traveling ship loader does the job of creating an even and balanced load in the ore boat.

Instead of dozens of mines on the list, there were only three mines shipping on the C&NW route by 1990. This resulted in just five different types of ore (pellets) and tailings being shipped through the Escanaba ore dock.

In many respects, the ore train operations were much simpler, but no less exciting. Furthermore, observing the C&NW ore operations invoked many memories of past operations even though the latest power for the road included SD50s instead of the Alcos, and SD18s and

GP38-2s for the yard operations. The same held true for the brief Union Pacific operation until the purchase of UP's former C&NW ore lines by the Wisconsin Central in 1997.

ROAD OPERATIONS

The 1990s-era road operations were dramatically different from the early 1970s. Instead of three- and four-unit Alco road switcher combinations for power, SD50s and GE Dash 8s performed the over-the-road hauls between Escanaba and the Marquette Range.

What was once a single ore train per day, if lucky, between Escanaba and Ishpeming, grew to

C&NW ore dock No. 6 at Escanaba, Michigan. The foundation of dock No. 5 can still be seen to the right. At one time there were four timber ore docks in operation at Escanaba. The Milwaukee Road had built two such docks near the C&NW facilities, but these were dismantled after the two roads entered into an ore-traffic pool agreement in the 1930s. C&NW, PATRICK C. DORIN COLLECTION

RIGHT: A trio of Fairbanks-Morse H-16-66 "Baby Train Masters" leads an Escanaba-bound trainload of iron ore pellets. The loads originated at the Groveland Mine, near Iron Mountain, Michigan. Since this is a C&NW-Milwaukee Road pooled ore train, the consist is a mixture of C&NW and Milwaukee Road ore cars with side extensions. ROBERT C. ANDERSON

BELOW AND OPPOSITE BOTTOM: Which railroad handled both Minnesota and Michigan ores through its ore dock? The answer, of course, is the Chicago & North Western, and subsequently the Union Pacific and Wisconsin Central following the merger and the WC's eventual purchase of ex-C&NW trackage. Led by SD50 No. 7016, a C&NW ore extra heads south to Rice Lake and a connection with the Wisconsin Central in 1992. Prior to the WC purchase, C&NW/UP ore trains operated to Rice Lake, and the Wisconsin Central handled the trains eastward to the connection near Escanaba. The four-unit power consist includes three C&NW units, and one WC unit still in Burlington Northern green. The extra train is at South Itasca on former CStPM&O (Omaha Road) trackage. BOTH, PATRICK C. DORIN COLLECTION

three or four trains per day depending upon the days of the week. There was actually more tonnage and train traffic rolling over the Escanaba–Ishpeming rail segment in 1995 than there had been in 1970. In terms of train traffic, however, it was about equal to that of the late 1950s when the C&NW handled a through freight train on a daily basis, plus two sets of passenger trains: the *Peninsula 400* and the *Iron and Copper Country Express*.

With the single ore train, there were four trains in each direction on a daily basis. The Chicago & North Western in the 1990s saw an equal amount but it was virtually all "ore" business. There was also a local train serving the freight business but this train did not operate on a daily basis in 1995.

The ore train business, however, has not been simply "ore train" operations.

The C&NW/UP also handled limestone for the pelletizing plants. The cars were delivered to the Lake Superior & Ishpeming Railroad at Eagle Mills or Partridge. The LS&I delivered the limestone loads to the Empire and Tilden mines for the creation of fluxed pellets. At the same time, empty C&NW ore cars were interchanged with the LS&I for movement to the Tilden mine for pellets destined to the Escanaba dock.

The C&NW did not handle mine run operations on the Marquette Range as the company did on the Menominee and the Gogebic Ranges. Until the C&NW became more of a participant in the movement of Marquette Range ore traffic, all C&NW ore trains were operated to Ishpeming, where the empties were interchanged with the LS&I.

A typical Chicago & North Western ore train in the 1990s consisted of about 100 or

Right: On August 6, 1996, Union Pacific 3842 North departed Ore Dock Yard (Escanaba) for a run north to the Empire Mine. Upon arrival at the mine, shown here, the crew set out the cars, which were loaded and prepared for the trip back to the ore dock the following day. PATRICK C. DORIN

Below: The crew has moved back to the trailing unit, which became the lead engine for the loaded movement back to Escanaba. With No. 5054 on the point, the crew was in the process of switching and coupling 54 loads to a group of 57 loads to make up their 111-car train. UP 5054 South will be ready to begin its journey to the Ore Dock within an hour. PATRICK C. DORIN

FACING PAGE: A Union Pacific ore train departs the Empire Mine on July 8, 1995. DAVID C. SCHAUER

more ore cars. The trains operated over what was known as the Partridge Subdivision. Each train was called a "turn," with the crews going north with the empties and limestone loads, and returning with loaded ore cars. A round trip took from five to ten hours, depending upon train traffic, weather, and other factors such as maintenance work.

Although the Republic Mine was no longer producing iron ore pellets for shipment, tailings were still being shipped to cement plants in Michigan during the 1990s. The C&NW and UP delivered empties to the LS&I at Ishpeming for movement to Republic. A cut of loaded cars from the Republic Mine has been delivered to the C&NW by the LS&I at the Ishpeming Yard in September 1984. PATRICK C. DORIN

Ore operations during the 1990s became even more interesting as limestone was shipped to Escanaba for movement to the pelletizing plants, creating a two-way move for the railroad and an improved iron ore product (fluxed pellets) for the steel industry. The method then used for limestone unloading was far from ideal, as it destroyed the extensions over time. PATRICK C. DORIN

Still another inbound traffic movement for pellet production is Bentonite clay. Note the "CNW" reporting marks on this UP covered hopper. PATRICK C. DORIN

THE ESCANABA ORE DOCK OPERATIONS

The new Escanaba ore dock was built on the site of the former No. 6 wooden ore dock. The wooden dock was dismantled in 1968, with the new dock going into operation for the 1969 shipping season.

The ore operations in 2002 under Wisconsin Central were practically identical. Upon arrival of a loaded train, the cars were inspected and then moved in blocks to the car dumper. There was one ore dock switch crew on duty two or three shifts per day depending upon traffic levels. The crew spotted the train at the dumper, and from that point on an automatic train positioner moved each block of cars through the rotary dumper.

After dumping, the cars rolled out of the dumping facility into the ore yard where again they were inspected for bad orders, etc. Some empties were moved to the coal dock facility to the north of the ore dock for limestone loading.

When the cars are unloaded, the pellets are moved by conveyor belt to a specific place in the ore dock storage area. Since 1990, there have been only three mines shipping five different products. The Tilden and Empire mines both ship fluxed and standard pellets with Republic shipping tailings or special orders. Fluxed pellets are different from each mine as are the standard pellets. Thus the five different products which must be stored separately.

Boat arrivals are scheduled well in advance. As the ore carrier ties up at the dock, the bucket reclaimer begins the task of scooping up the particular pellets consigned to that boat. The pellets are then placed on the conveyor belt for movement to the dock. They are weighed before being deposited into the boat. When the appropriate tonnage has been loaded, the process stops and the vessel departs for ports on Lake Michigan and Lake Erie.

During some winter seasons in the 1990s, Inland Steel Company shipped pellets from its Minorca Plant on the Mesabi Range to the Escanaba ore dock. Originally, the ore was handled by the DM&IR to the C&NW at South Itasca (Superior), Wisconsin. The C&NW then

The No. 6 wooden dock at Escanaba was replaced by a low level ore dock in 1969. This early 1970s aerial view shows the new dock, as well as the extent of stockpiled iron ore pellets from both the Marquette and Menominee Ranges. CHICAGO & NORTH WESTERN, PATRICK C. DORIN COLLECTION

The C&NW's wooden ore dock No. 6 at Escanaba is in full operation in this September 1965 view. A Milwaukee Road F-M H-16-66 is spotting a 30-car "shove" atop the dock. KAREN M. DORIN

This view shows the pocket arrangement atop the ore dock. F-M H-16-66 No. 1670 is spotting a cut of both C&NW and Milwaukee Road ore cars without extensions. The F-M was built in 1953 but is shown here in the later simplified paint scheme. Incidently, the top of the No. 6 ore dock was very similar to the wooden ore docks owned and operated by the C&NW in Ashland. C&NW, PATRICK C. DORIN COLLECTION

interchanged the loaded trains with the Wisconsin Central near Rice Lake, Wisconsin. The WC handled the trains to a connection with the C&NW at Hermansville, Michigan—west of Escanaba. Consequently, a sixth and separate product was and is handled at the Escanaba dock. C&NW ore cars were used for this service, and this was still true on the Wisconsin Central/CN until 2002 (see Chapter 3).

The C&NW dock at Escanaba is 1900 feet long, and is the only low-level dock of its kind on the Great Lakes. The dock facility has a storage capacity of two million tons of iron ore pellets. Since the new dock replaced the former wooden dock No. 6, the facility has retained its No. 6 designation. However, there are no other docks in the Escanaba area.

In a way, it is hard to imagine that at various times throughout the 20th century, the Soo Line, the Milwaukee Road, and the Chicago & North Western maintained ore docks in this important lake port comprising the cities of Escanaba and Gladstone. The maximum number of ore docks here at any one time was four.

The "Ore Dock" station sign is at the north end of the ore yard facility.

The No. 5 ore dock foundations can still be seen in Lake Michigan just to the north of the low-level dock.

A rare day when three boats were tied up at the C&NW dock for loading. An Inland Steel boat is at right—Inland Steel ships a major portion of their pellets from their plant in Minnesota during the winter, in order to get a jump start on the movement of iron ore supplies at their Indiana Harbor plant in the spring. ALL, PATRICK C. DORIN

Entrance to the ore car dumper at the Escanaba dock in 1996.

The ore is dumped three cars at a time. When dumping is completed, the cut of three cars rolls out of the dumping shed to a yard track for eventual switching into a northbound empty train for the Marquette Range.

After dumping, the iron ore pellets either move directly to a ship by conveyor belt or to a stockpile for a particular type of ore. Pellets moving toward the dock go through this overflow protector to ensure an even flow of pellets for movement through the ship loader and into a vessel.
ALL, PATRICK C. DORIN

A cut of ex-C&NW ore cars being shoved toward the ore dock approach in 1996. There were 51 cars in this Union Pacific shove to the ore dock.

UP 6115 is working fairly hard as it moves the ore cars upgrade while moving over the street crossing at the north end of the yard.

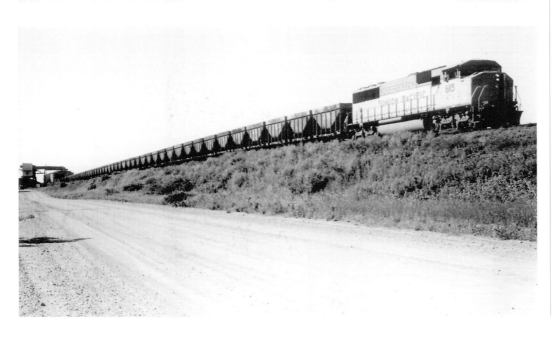

No. 6115 is coming close to the destination where the train will be spotted for movement through the car dumper. As soon as the spotting is completed, the ore dock assignment will be uncoupled and return to the yard for any switching that needs to be done for a new empty train, or to pick up another group of loads for the dumping operation. ALL, PATRICK C. DORIN

ALL-RAIL ORE MOVEMENT

The Chicago & North Western particpated in the all-rail movement of iron ore from the Mesabi and Marquette Ranges beginning in the 1950s. The ore movements from the Marquette Range have been minimal, and what traffic there was traveled straight down to Chicago. The routes from the Mesabi Range, however, have been far more varied with wider assortments of motive power and rolling stock.

One of the most important movements of iron ore pellet—and one of the longest-lasting in terms of traffic history—was the Geneva, Utah, "through-train" service with the Union Pacific. During the 1980s, and even into the early 1990s, the equipment consisted of 100-ton open-top hoppers and Union Pacific ore cars. By virtue of their merger into the UP, equipment from both the Missouri Pacific and Western Pacific was also part of the consists of these massive and heavy trains. A variety of cabooses also appeared in C&NW, Missouri Pacific, Western Pacific, Southern Pacific, and Union Pacific colors.

Motive power displayed the same variations. It was almost like a "look into the future" when the C&NW would become part of the Union Pacific System in 1995.

Other all-rail movements consisted of ore trains made up of Duluth, Missabe & Iron Range ore cars for movement from Superior, Wisconsin, to the Chicago and Pittsburgh areas. DM&IR motive power often ran through with the 100- to 110-car trains, which were inter-

All-rail ore movements on the C&NW during the 1970s involved trains from the DM&IR. SD40 No. 882 leads a 100-car train of DM&IR ore cars loaded with taconite pellets for a connection with the Elgin, Joliet & Eastern Railway for movement to Gary, Indiana. The train is departing Itasca Yard on the far east side of Superior, Wisconsin, in January 1973.

The second unit on the train is a leased Norfolk & Western C-628, later purchased by the C&NW for ore service. BOTH, PATRICK C. DORIN

All-rail ore trains over the C&NW during the 1970s were also handled by DM&IR motive power. In this trio of photos, a northbound (C&NW westbound) empty ore train is powered by three DM&IR SD9s. Thus this train is designated as "Extra DM&IR 120 West."

The train consisted of 100 empty DM&IR ore cars.

Bringing up the rear was a C&NW bay-window caboose. The train departed Rockmount Siding, about nine miles south of Itasca on the Itasca Subdivision, after a meet with an eastbound time freight to the Twin Cities. Extra DM&IR 120 West will tie up in Itasca yard and a DM&IR transfer will arrive from Proctor, Minnesota, later in the afternoon to pick up the empties. ALL, PATRICK C. DORIN

changed with the Elgin, Joliet & Eastern Railway in the Chicago area for movement to the Norfolk & Western and other eastern carriers.

There is an interesting sidelight to these Chicago-bound ore trains. Because of bridge problems near Eau Claire, the C&NW originally routed their all-rail ore trains from Superior to Spooner and then to Hudson, Wisconsin, over the former Omaha Road. At Hudson, the trains turned eastward over the main line to the Chicago area. The empty trains were routed to Eau Claire and then turned north to Spooner and Superior. The C&NW subsequently abandoned the route from Spooner to Hudson, as well as its main line from Superior to Rice Lake, and began running all trains over the Burlington Northern between Superior and the Twin Cities. This included both ore trains and regular C&NW freight traffic.

The Union Pacific still handles Geneva all-rail ore trains as we move into the 21st century. Since the UP has absorbed the C&NW, Rio Grande, and Southern Pacific through merger, it is a single-line haul from the DM&IR and Superior all the way to Utah. The Geneva trains operate over former Great Northern trackage from Saunders (south of Superior) to St. Paul, and via Union Pacific trackage the rest of the way.

JACKSON COUNTY ALL-RAIL

The only Wisconsin iron mine in operation in recent years was the Jackson County Iron Company near Black River Falls.

In 1992 the C&NW purchased a 500-car fleet of DM&IR ore cars. They were re-stenciled with "CNW" reporting marks and new numbers, and used immediately in some of the all-rail ore services.

C&NW Black River Falls 100-ton ore cars were also used in all-rail service. Such a train is shown here at Itasca yard in the early 1990s.

The variety of power from the UP system in the mid- to late 1990s was matched by the range of cabooses used in all-rail ore service. Former Western Pacific bay window caboose No. 435 was at Itasca in this view. ALL, PATRICK C. DORIN

A Union Pacific all-rail empty has arrived at South Itasca on the Wisconsin Central on July 25, 1999. The power consists of both UP and SP diesels. Lead unit No. 8019, an SD90MAC, is typical of the UP's all-rail Geneva ore train power moving into the 21st century.

A westbound UP all-rail is moving over the DM&IR's Interstate Branch en route from Itasca to Steelton Yard on November 8, 1999. DM&IR crews will take the train to Minntac to load pellets for the Geneva plant in Utah. Note the wide variety of coal hoppers in ore service, such as the Rio Grande car in the lead, followed by a Chicago Heights Terminal Transfer Railroad, another subsidiary of the Union Pacific. ROBERT BLOMQUIST

Two UP units lead a C&NW engine on an empty Geneva all-rail train en route to the DM&IR's Steelton Yard on April 12, 2000. The train is approaching Saunders (just south of Superior), an important connection for many of the Superior-area railroads including BNSF, Canadian Pacific, Union Pacific, Canadian National (Duluth, Winnipeg & Pacific), DM&IR, and Wisconsin Central. ROBERT BLOMQUIST

This company began operations in the early 1970s and closed in 1983. The mine and pellet plant produced about 700,000 tons annually, which was shipped in the newest of the Chicago & North Western 100-ton ore cars to the Inland Steel Plant at Indiana Harbor, Indiana. This traffic was handled in regular freight trains between the mine and the interchange with the Indiana Harbor Belt Railroad, which delivered the loads to the steel plant.

There has not been a single iron ore mine operating in the State of Wisconsin since Jackson

County closed in 1983. The C&NW ore cars, built specifically for the Jackson County operation, were placed in other train services including all-rail movements and rock and stone traffic.

THE C&NW ORE CAR FLEET

Most of the North Western ore car fleet has consisted of tapered-side, 70-ton equipment with side extensions since the 1970s. The 50-ton cars

were gone by the early 1970s.

The cars have taken on a variety of colors and lettering, among the most attractive being those rebuilt during the 1980s and painted green. In addition, the C&NW purchased a fleet of 70-ton ore cars from the Duluth, Missabe & Iron Range which have seen a variety of services including rock and stone traffic.

The North Western also owned a fleet of ex-Bessemer & Lake Erie ore cars, which were similar to the Lake Superior design. As of 2001, many cars were still carrying their CNW report-

FINAL C&NW ORE CAR ROSTER — 1995

Number Series	Qty.	Capacity	Remarks
2261-3010	103	77 Tons	No extensions
110500-110606	77	100 Tons	35' 11" long, Black River Falls cars
112000-112611	434	77 Tons	18" extensions
113501-114499	71	77 Tons	Odd numbers
118601-119099	186	77 Tons	18" extensions Odd numbers
122401-122699	122	77 Tons	18" extensions Odd numbers
122700-123040	110	77 Tons	
810000-810499	500	77 Tons	Ex-DM&IR

C&NW No. 119063—note the placement of the reporting marks and the insignia. PATRICK C. DORIN

No. 2711 was rebuilt in 1977 and photographed on July 1, 1979, at the Humboldt Mine west of Ishpeming. ROBERT C. ANDERSON

A 1969 view of No. 122986, rebuilt in 1967 with 18-inch extensions for handling pellets, and painted in a somewhat lighter box car red with yellow lettering. PATRICK C. DORIN

No. 118947 was rebuilt at Clinton in April 1976. The car was still painted red with white lettering and the "Employee Owned" insignia at Escanaba in 1980. PATRICK C. DORIN

No. 112118R was part of a group of ore cars rebuilt in 1985 and painted green with yellow lettering. PATRICK C. DORIN

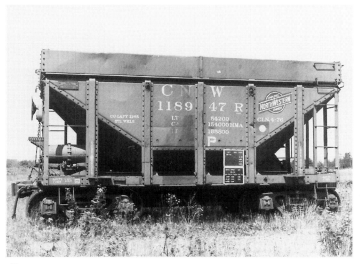

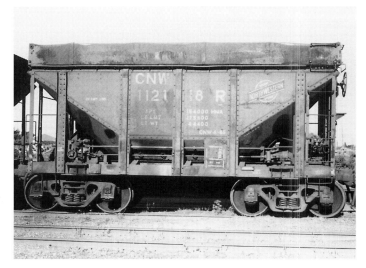

Another view of a green ore car, in this instance No. 112231. This group was originally built by Bethlehem Steel in 1955.

C&NW ore car No. 122973, at the Escanaba Ore Yard in 1995. BOTH, PATRICK C. DORIN

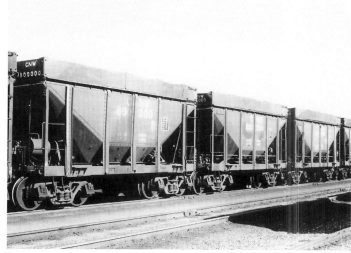

No. 2847, at Eagle Mills on August 24, 1996, was part of the last group of 70-ton ore cars built for the C&NW in the mid-1950s.

Triple ore cars—all numbered 800000—were semi-permanently coupled as an experiment. The company did not continue the practice, as the three-car 800000 caused confusion on Wisconsin Central. Escanaba, 1996.

No. 120046, at Escanaba in 1996, is an ex-DM&IR 75-ton ore car.

No. 810328 is one of the 500-car fleet purchased from the DM&IR in 1992. Paint was box car red with a black panel for the new lettering.

No. 800126 is a rebuilt ex-LS&I ore car in red with white lettering, at Escanaba in August 1996
ALL, PATRICK C. DORIN

ing marks but were being relettered SSAM for the Wisconsin Central ore train services.

C&NW ore trains can be modeled using HO-scale Model Die Casting tapered-side ore cars.

MOTIVE POWER NOTES

C&NW ore trains were powered by 2-8-2s and 2-8-4s during the days of steam.

Electro-Motive Division F-units in two- to four-unit combinations handled ore trains during the 1950s, with generally a 50-car consist for each unit. When the F's went into passenger commuter service in Chicago, Fairbanks-Morse 1600-hp road switchers became the mainstay of C&NW ore-train power, often mixed with Milwaukee Road F-M road switchers. Electro-Motive GP7s and GP9s also operated in North Western ore service, including switching duties on the ore docks in Ashland. Milwaukee Road Geeps were also operated in the C&NW's ore territory.

The next phase of power in the 1970s saw Alcos arrive from the Norfolk & Western, which in turn were replaced by the SD's in the late 1980s and 1990s. Ore train lengths ranged from 60 or 70 cars to over 150 or 175 cars.

The ore trains with the greatest variety of equipment operated out of the Duluth-Superior area. With the exception of the ore trains consisting of DM&IR ore cars (powered by GP9s through GP40s and the heavy duty SD40-2s, etc.), the trains to the west had an almost unimaginable variety of motive power.

SELECTED ORE TONNAGES

C&NW docks at Escanaba (includes ore from Menominee, Marquette, and Gogebic Ranges):

1957	5,907,579	tons
1967	6,565,770	
1976	10,060,858	(Marquette increase)
1977	7,723,145	

The C&NW purchased a small fleet of ex-Bessemer & Lake Erie ore cars, like No. 121170, shown near Woodruff, Wisconsin, in August 1978. JOSEPH PIERSEN

C&NW scale test car No. 263629 was rebuilt from one of the 70-ton tapered-side ore cars.

Union Pacific 100-ton ore cars like No. 26596 operated on the C&NW for all-rail ore service.

UP 27059, another 100-ton hopper, was originally painted silver but dust and grime covered its lettering. A silver panel was painted on to refresh the car's reporting marks, numbering, and other data. THREE PHOTOS, PATRICK C. DORIN

Two examples of motive power operated by the C&NW at the Escanaba ore yard are SD18R No. 6637 and SD60 No. 8042, at Escanaba in 1995. The primary job of the SD18R was switching, while the SD60 handled the road ore trains. On rare occasions, a single SD60 would power a shorter ore train. PATRICK C. DORIN

Alco C-425 diesels were also found in ore service during the 1970s and 1980s. No. 4257 was previously numbered 403, and is shown here at Ishpeming between ore runs in the late 1970s. THOMAS A. DORIN

The Fairbank-Morse H-16-66s were replaced with ex-Norfolk & Western Alco C-628s as well as other units including the C-425s. Nos. 6712 and 6701 are laying over at Ishpeming after bringing in an empty ore train and are waiting for loads from the Lake Superior & Ishpeming Railroad. The C&NW operated the C-628s with the short end leading. The long end was actually the front end per N&W specifications. THOMAS A. DORIN

Even in the modern diesel era from the 1950s on, steam played a role in the North Western's iron ore services. The C&NW used one of its streamlined Hudsons for thawing ore at Ashland, Wisconsin. Prior to the construction of an ore car thawing plant at Escanaba, the C&NW employed two such Hudsons, displaced from their former passenger duties, for streaming frozen ore prior to its dumping on the wooden ore dock.
HAROLD K. VOLLRATH COLLECTION

GP40s and GP50s also graced the C&NW ore lines in Michigan. No. 5517 is shown here laying over at the LS&I Eagle Mills engine facility. The GP40s have been on the C&NW since 1980. PATRICK C. DORIN

Union Pacific power was the last to operate (before the WC) between Escanaba and the Marquette Iron Range. One example was the No. 6115, an SD60M, at Escanaba on August 6, 1996. This particular unit's assignment on this day was switching the ore yard and shoving loads to the car dumper.
PATRICK C. DORIN

ABOVE: During the spring of 2001, the WC-SSAM made a decision to rebuild 500 former-C&NW ore cars at the Fond du Lac shops. New draft gear, roller bearing inserts, side extensions, and maroon paint were among the major improvements. SSAM 2407, at Escanaba on June 28, 2001, illustrates the new WC maroon paint scheme as well as the roller bearings. PATRICK C. DORIN

FACING PAGE: It is a beautiful August day in 1998, and the SORE 3 (meaning Escanaba third ore train) is getting ready to depart the ore yard with an empty train for the Marquette Range.
PATRICK C. DORIN

The Wisconsin Central is the newest railroad name in the Lake Superior region—not counting of course, the Union Pacific which had taken over the Chicago & North Western Railway, and then sold the ore lines to the WC in 1997.

Not only is the WC the newest kid on the block, but the company has the widest variety of ore train operations of any rail line. And all of this has been accomplished during the company's first decade of existence.

The WC's ore operations can be divided into four categories (not including the Algoma Central, which is covered in Chapter 4).

BRIDGE COMPANY/
THE WISCONSIN CENTRAL

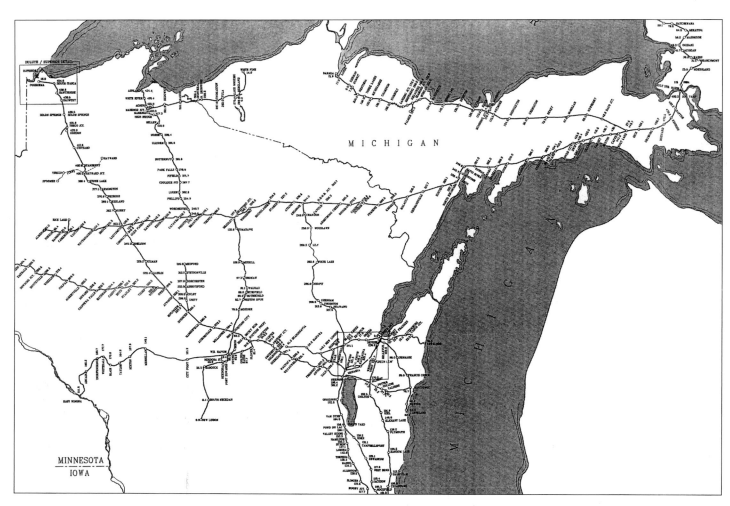

All-rail ore trains can have many surprises. An all-rail loaded DM&IR ore train for the Wisconsin Central is arriving at Steelton with three WC SD45s and one Soo Line SD40-2, the 6608. The DM&IR crew will hand the train over to a WC crew, who will take it over the Interstate Branch to the WC trackage southeast of Superior. PATRICK C. DORIN

An eastbound loaded all-rail Middletown ore train rolls along over the Superior Subdivison toward Stevens Point. The power consist includes an SD45, No. 6530, with an ex-BN SD45 following (still in BN colors) and CSX Dash 8-40CW No. 7744 topping off the trio. PATRICK C. DORIN

FACING PAGE: An empty all-rail ore train has arrived at South Itasca (Superior), Wisconsin, in August 1998 and the crew has tied up for the day. A transfer crew will handle the train over the DM&IR's Interstate Branch for delivery at the Steelton Yard in the Gary-New Duluth area. The DM&IR will forward the train to the Evtac Plant at Eveleth for loading and then return it to the WC. PATRICK C. DORIN

ALL-RAIL OPERATIONS

This was a major operation for the Wisconsin Central and included a wide variety of motive power and equipment. Most of the all-rail services operated between Steelton (Duluth) and Chicago. The Duluth, Missabe & Iron Range Railway delivered unit trains to the WC for a number of destinations, including Chicago, Alabama, and other eastern steel centers.

Motive power configurations on the all-rail ore trains have included locomotives painted for CSX, Norfolk Southern, Union Pacific, Southern Pacific, Rio Grande, C&NW, DM&IR, as well as Wisconsin Central's own locomotives. Conrail motive power has also been part of the picture. This is another example of the wide diversity of motive power and equipment on the ore lines. The ore-carrying equipment includes CSX, SP, UP, Rio Grande, Conrail, NS, C&NW, B&LE

and BN 100-ton hopper cars. The mixtures of motive power and equipment will depend upon the destinations, such as the Fairfield Works or Gary Works. In fact, trains en route to Gary Works were often made up of DM&IR ore cars.

The WC has also handled all-rail ore from the Marquette Range. Prior to the purchase of the C&NW ore lines, such trains were routed from Eagle Mills eastward to Trout Lake and then westward back to Gladstone and Argonne. Turning south to Chicago, the trains were then interchanged with various connecting carriers depending the destination of the all-rail ore trains. These ore movements were the last major train operations east of Marquette, Michigan, on the former Duluth, South Shore & Atlantic Railroad line. Since the purchase of the C&NW ore lines, any all-rail ore traffic moves south via Escanaba and Green Bay to the Chicago interchanges.

Sometimes WC power could be mixed with units from the Union Pacific system, as in this WC-UP-SP trio laying over between all-rail ore assignments at the ex-C&NW terminal at Itasca in mid-2000.

Here are four examples of all-rail hoppers seen in ore service on the Wisconsin Central. WC 343077 is an ex-Clinchfield quad hopper .

No. 812633 is one of many CSX hoppers to visit the WC.

As cars are repainted from their previous owner, the new WC all-rail cars receive either WC or SSAM reporting marks. SSAM 30119 was photographed in Spring 1998.

CSX hoppers with NYC reporting marks began to appear after the 1999 split of Conrail between CSX and Norfolk Southern. Ex-Conrail rolling stock acquired by CSX received the venerable NYC identification. ALL, PATRICK C. DORIN

MESABI RANGE TO ESCANABA

No one would ever have guessed that one day Mesabi ore would be moving east to Escanaba. Such has been the case for several years with the WC handling Minorca pellets to Escanaba during the winter months. The pellets are stockpiled, and shipped to Indiana Harbor, Indiana, via boat during the spring season. The reason for such a routing is to get a "jump start" on the lake shipping of ore to Inland Steel.

When the operations first started, the C&NW still existed and operated its own railroad line south from Superior to Eau Claire, Wisconsin—a long-time route for many all-rail ore trains. The DM&IR originally interchanged the Minorca pellets with the C&NW at Itasca (East Superior). The C&NW handled the trains south to Rice Lake and Cameron and interchanged the trains with the WC. The trains operated eastward from Cameron to Hermansville, where they were turned over to the

C&NW for the remainder of the journey to Escanaba.

The C&NW eventually gave up their operations on the Eau Claire line and secured trackage rights over the WC from Superior to Nekoosa, Wisconsin. When this happened the WC eventually took over the operation of the trains to Escanaba. And now, since the WC owns the former C&NW lines and ore handling facilities, it is a WC and DM&IR interchange movement from northern Minnesota to northern Michigan with the longest mine-to-lake port operation now in existence. The Minorca trains are made up of C&NW ore cars with extensions. As of the spring of 1999, none of the C&NW cars had been relettered either WC or SSAM (the latter are the Sault Ste. Marie Bridge Company reporting marks).The ore cars began receiving SSAM reporting marks in 2000.

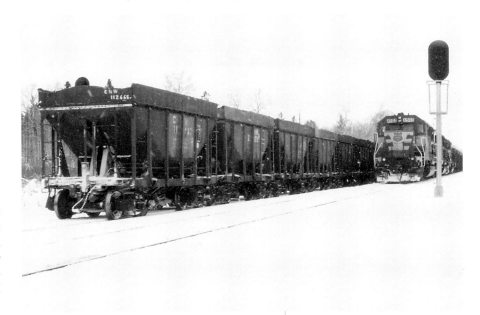

MARQUETTE RANGE TO ESCANABA

The former C&NW ore train operations served two mines on the Marquette Range. The empty ore trains move north en route to either the Empire Mine directly or to the LS&I at Eagle Mills for empties destined for the Tilden Mine. The LS&I delivers the empties for loading at the Tilden and returns the loads to Partridge for the SSAM crews to make up the loaded train and return to Escanaba.

The SSAM trains upon arrival at the Empire Mine, spot the empty cars for loading. Loaded cars are then assembled for the movement back to Escanaba. Both the SSAM and LS&I can switch the Empire Mine, whereas only the LS&I handles the Tilden Mine.

Limestone for fluxing pellets has also been handled by the SSAM from Escanaba to the Marquette Range.

During normal business levels, there are three to four ore trains per day dispatched to the Marquette Range with 108 cars. This will vary depending upon the number of limestone loads going north. Loaded trains going south have comprised as few as 50 cars, again depending upon the scheduling or trains.

The Republic Mine, although not producing any pellets, does from time to time ship special ores. At one time, tailings or rock from the

Mesabi Range ore trains from the Minorca pelletizing plant and mine en route to Escanaba were powered by a variety of WC power including the SD45s throughout the 1990s. An empty Minorca train arrives at South Itasca while a southbound freight waits for the ore train to clear in January 1999. PATRICK C. DORIN

DM&IR motive power also did the honors on the WC Minorca ore trains. Two DM&IR units are shown here leading a train out of the Steelton Yard and bound for South Itasca in January 1998. MICHAEL BURLAGA

In February 2001, the Minorca trains were powered by borrowed CSX units like No. 801. This train is about to depart South Itasca for Escanaba. PATRICK C. DORIN

Algoma Steel is now one of the primary users of Marquette Range iron ore pellets since the mine at Wawa, Ontario, closed in 1998. This August 1998 view shows a cut of Green Bay & Western ore cars loaded with rock being switched at Steelton (Sault Ste. Marie), Ontario—not to be confused with the Steelton at Duluth, Minnesota. The GB&W ore cars are identical to the group of red cars owned by the Lake Superior & Ishpeming Railroad. PATRICK C. DORIN

mine was shipped to Lower Michigan for cement processing, but this has not happened since the mid- to late 1990s.

Any traffic for the SSAM is interchanged with the LS&I at Eagle Mills. Although it is stretching the words a bit, it can be said that the SSAM is still serving three mines on the Marquette Range.

THE MARQUETTE RANGE TO ALGOMA STEEL

The year 1998 saw new developments in the movement of ore from the Marquette Range. The mine and processing plant at Wawa, Ontario, closed. New contracts were signed, and Algoma Steel now receives their iron ore pellets from the Tilden Mine on the Marquette Range

via the SSAM and the Wisconsin Central routing from Eagle Mills to Gladstone and then eastward to Sault Ste. Marie, Ontario. These trains consist of the former Algoma Central 100-ton ore cars or 100-ton coal hopper cars, adding a new dimension to the railroad operations on the original Soo Line between Gladstone and Sault Ste. Marie. The Algoma ore traffic adds still another train to the traffic density on the former C&NW ore lines, which now see more train traffic than ever—since the days of the *Peninsula 400* and the *Iron and Copper Country Express* passenger trains.

THE ESCANABA ORE DOCK

The C&NW replaced its wooden ore dock in 1969 with a low-level dock equipped with a traveling ship loader. This dock is able to load any type of ore carrier operated on the Great Lakes.

The ore-dumping process is fairly simple. The loaded ore cars are pulled from the yard tracks and spotted at the dumper. An automatic train positioner moves the set of cars through the dumper, three at a time. The rotary system turns the cars over, dumps the contents, returns the cars to the upright position, and releases them as empties back to the ore yard. The pellets then move by a conveyor system to the appropriate storage area for each type of pellet.

The ore-dock unloading facility was modified in early 2001 to handle hopper dumping for DM&IR ore cars as well as 100-ton-capacity hopper cars.

FUTURE PROSPECTS

The Wisconsin Central has built a solid and positive reputation for the movement of iron ore from the Mesabi and Marquette iron ranges. The company is always looking for new ways to provide service for the mining companies. One example was a proposal for Northshore Mining Company in Silver Bay, Minnesota, to ship their pellets by boat across Lake Superior to Ashland, Wisconsin. There the pellets would be loaded into railroad cars for all-rail movements to a variety of destinations. This would bring iron ore traffic back through Ashland for the first time since 1965.

As we moved into the 21st century, the WC had the widest variety of ore train operations to be found anywhere. It was an incredible operation with far-reaching benefits for all of North

Two WC SD45s were working Escanaba's morning ore dock assignment on August 4, 1998. Even with most of the trains receiving one type of iron product from either the Tilden or Empire Mine, there is still some yard work to do. This includes spotting the loads for the dumper, switching out the "bad orders," and building the empty trains for movement back to the Marquette Range. This also includes adding Bentonite and limestone loads for the mines.

This WC switch crew, with a pair of SD45s at their disposal, is pulling the empties from the Escanaba dumper.

The boat for August 4, 1998, had not yet arrived at the WC-SSAM Escanaba ore dock when this photo was taken. ALL, PATRICK C. DORIN

The dumper station at the Escanaba ore dock yard in August 1998.

WC covered hopper cars with Soo Line lettering are spotted at the dumper for dust collection from the unloading of iron ore pellets.
BOTH, PATRICK C. DORIN

America. The company was to be commended for its transportation of iron ore—mine-to-dock, all-rail, and beyond!

THE WC AND SSAM ORE LINES

The ore lines extended from the Marquette Range to the Escanaba ore dock facility as well as eastward to Sault Ste. Marie, Ontario, via Gladstone. All-rail routes extend south from both Superior and Escanaba.

The only railroad reaching into the Gogebic Range territory is the former DSS&A line from Marengo Junction, Wisconsin, to the White Pine Mine located northeast of Bessemer.

The Sault Ste. Marie Bridge Company had this interesting sign at the Escanaba ore dock yard in August 1998.

This June 2001 ore dock job has been assigned some testing with newly rebuilt and repainted Ortner ore cars from the Algoma Central. Wisconsin Central SD45 No. 7500 is coupled to caboose No. 17, which has been outfitted for Remote Control work.
BOTH, PATRICK C. DORIN

The Wisconsin Central's subsidiary, the Sault Ste. Marie Bridge Company, acquired the C&NW fleet of ore cars when it purchased the C&NW lines north of Green Bay. Most of the ore cars are so stained from iron ore and limestone dust that the reporting marks have been almost blotted out as shown here with ex-C&NW No. 112138.

Many of the C&NW rebuilt ore cars were repainted in their green color scheme, such as the 112194, shown in August 1998.

CNW ore car 2272 is virtually identical to the Model Die Casting HO-scale tapered-side car. Note the "R" to the right of the number, indicating a rebuilt car. The side extensions take a beating during the unloading process for limestone at the mines.

The C&NW purchased a number of somewhat newer ore cars from the LS&I. Note the paint job and the 800134 numbering in this view at Escanaba in August 1998. This equipment does not have the same type of top lip as the other C&NW cars. It is fairly easy to distinguish the ex-LS&I cars by the type of extension. Note also the braces on the side of the extension.
ALL, PATRICK C. DORIN

During the spring of 2001, the WC-SSAM made a decision to rebuild 500 of the ex-C&NW ore cars. The cars went through an extensive rebuilding process at Wisconsin Central's Fond du Lac shops, receiving new draft gears, rolling bearings, extensions, and a new maroon paint job. The fleet of 500 rebuilt ore cars actually covers three variations. SSAM 2569 represents the last new group of C&NW ore cars built in 1955 by Bethlehem Steel. Note the grooved ribs at each end of the car, at Escanaba on June 28, 2001.

SSAM 3256, at Escanaba on June 28, 2001, is a rebuild of a former Lake Superior & Ishpeming car. It is a newer design, without the lip at the top of the car. Note the braced extension.

SSAM 208472, at Escanaba on June 27, 2001, is a former Algoma Central ore car built by Ortner. These cars were painted a light gray with a "Wisconsin Central System" insignia and SSAM reporting marks.

SSAM 208093 is part of the fleet of ex-Algoma Central "bathtub"-type ore cars that have emerged in this light gray WC scheme. The car was photographed in June 2001 at the connection between the SSAM and the E&LS at Iron Mountain, Michigan. ALL, PATRICK C. DORIN

An empty train departs the Escanaba ore yard for Eagle Mills and interchange with the LS&I for loading at the Tilden Mine on June 28, 2001. The LS&I will return the loads to the SSAM at Partridge. The loaded train will then head for Algoma Steel at Sault Ste. Marie, Ontario. The covered hopper on the head-end of the 46-car train is loaded with clay for the taconite pellet plants. PATRICK C. DORIN

SSAM TRAIN OPERATIONS ON AUGUST 3, 1998

The train symbol "SORE" means Escanaba Ore.

SORE 1   6:00 a.m.
With freight to Eagle Mills and 108 empties
Return with 108 loads

SORE 2   12:01 p.m.
With 50 limestones to spot and 54 empties
Return with 108 loads

SORE 3   6:00 p.m.
With clay to spot and pull.
108 empties
Return with 108 loads

SORE 4   11:30 p.m.
With 50 limestone to spot and 54 empties
Return with 108 loads

THE ORE CAR FLEET

Phase 1—1998
All C&NW ore cars with original number series

Phase 2—2000
Relettering of C&NW ore cars with SSAM reporting marks. New number series: 2300s to 2800s.

Phase 3—2001
Rebuilding 500 ex-C&NW and ex-LS&I ore cars including repainting in the WC maroon and SSAM reporting marks within the number series listed above (the number series may be expanded as time goes on).

CANADIAN NATIONAL PURCHASES THE WC

The Wisconsin Central was purchased by Canadian National in 2001, with some modifications to the operation in 2002 due to the economy.

Wisconsin Central local freight symbol L045 was approaching Saxon, Wisconsin, in July 2001 en route to Marengo Junction for a connection with the Ashland–Mellen–Stevens Point freight trains. The 30-car train includes eight cars of iron ore from the Peterson Mine at Bessemer on the Gogebic Range. The ore is being shipped to a paint manufacturer, which has been purchasing the remains of the stockpile for several years. Since the original WC line from Mellen to Bessemer has been torn up, the stockpiled ore must now be trucked to the WC's ex-DSS&A main line at Thomaston, Michigan. It is then loaded into ex-Milwaukee Road gondola cars for shipment to the paint company. Since mining ceased on the Gogebic Range in 1968, it can be said—for the moment anyway—that this is the last remaining ore operation on the Gogebic Range. JOEL NAGRO

4 ALGOMA CENTRAL

ABOVE: Algoma Central operated two styles of modern 100-ton ore cars. One was an outside braced car with end platforms, such as No. 8482 illustrated here. These cars were transferred to the Wisconsin Central after mining ceased at Wawa, Ontario, and they now carry WC initials.
PATRICK C. DORIN

FACING PAGE: Lettered and renumbered for its new owner, former Algoma Central SD40-2 No. 6005 leads a three-unit lashup on an AC ore train at Wawa, Ontario, in February 1995. Wawa is located on the branch line between Hawk Junction and Michipicoten. STEVE GLISCHINSKI

The Algoma Central Railway has been an ore hauler for most of its history. An ore dock was built at Michipicoten Harbour, Ontario, at the end of a branch line serving Wawa, the location of an iron ore mine. This mine shipped ore all-rail over the Algoma Central on a daily basis to the Algoma Steel Works at Sault Ste. Marie, Ontario, as well as some shipments through the ore dock on Lake Superior.

Sadly, these operations came to an end in June 1998, when the mine at Wawa closed permanently.

The consist of the daily all-rail train included 100-ton-capacity jumbo ore hoppers. When the Wisconsin Central purchased the AC, the ore cars were renumbered and relettered with WC reporting marks. Since the mine at Wawa closed, the cars have

been transferred to the Wisconsin Central for other traffic.

The ore dock was owned and operated by Landfill Mining Limited. It had two conveyor systems capable of handling 2000 tons per hour with one loader, and 4000 tons per hour with two loaders. The dock facility included a ground storage capacity of 500,000 gross tons.

When the current dock was constructed in 1939, it replaced a pocket-type dock which was quite different from the other ore docks on Lake Superior and Michigan.

The original ACR ore cars also were similar, but not identical, to most of the Lake Superior ore cars. The modern ore car fleet replaced all of the smaller cars by the 1970s.

One group designated as ore cars was numbered 8001 to 8100. The 100-ton capacity cars were 43 feet, 7 inches long with 2200 cubic feet of capacity.

The railroad also took delivery of 300 rapid-discharge cars numbered 8201 to 8500 in 1974 and 1975. These 100-ton cars were 43 feet, 10 inches long with a 2100-cubic-foot capacity. Both sets of cars were painted a dark green, which in some cases later appeared to be black.

The Algoma Central served the mine at Wawa. Two ACR Geeps are switching cars at the mine in this late-1950s view. ALGOMA CENTRAL

Part of the ore mined was shipped to Michipicoten Harbour. Note the ore piles stored in the background of this 1950s scene for transloading to ships for movement to Sault Ste. Marie and other Great Lakes destinations. ALGOMA CENTRAL

Other business on the Algoma Central includes a through freight train in each direction on a daily basis. Freight traffic grew during the late 1990s and was one source of through traffic for Wisconsin Central symbol freights SOGBA and GBSOA between Green Bay, Wisconsin, and Sault Ste. Marie, Ontario.

One very interesting aspect of the Algoma Central has been its passenger train service. The company operates a through passenger train (Numbers 1 and 2) between Sault Ste. Marie and Hearst, Ontario. The schedule varies with the seasons—four times per week in the summer and three times weekly in the winter. The consists of trains 1 and 2 typically range from three to five cars.

The ACR has become world famous for its Agawa Canyon Tour Train. This train operates on a daily basis during the summer between Sault Ste. Marie and rugged Agawa Canyon. The

The destination for most of the ore mined on the Algoma Central was the Algoma Steel Company in Sault Ste. Marie, Ontario. A Canada Steamship Lines vessel was unloading there in September 1979. KEVIN J. HOLLAND

This July 1965 view shows the Algoma Steel docks in the lower section of the photo, while the ACR rail yards are located above the steel works and to the right. ALGOMA CENTRAL

The most recent Algoma Central ore trains consisted of the heavy 100-ton capacity cars, as shown here behind SD40-2 No. 6005 east of Wawa.
STEVE GLISCHINSKI

The heart of the iron ore movement are the ore trains themselves. This photo was taken from ACR passenger train No. 1 (en route to Hearst) at Hawk Junction in October 1973. The three ACR Geeps on the right are switching loaded ore cars for movement to Sault Ste. Marie. GORDON D. JOMINI

consist of the tour train can range upwards of 20 cars. Equipment includes one or two dining cars, a dome-lounge car (a former Union Pacific car), and as many coaches as needed to accommodate the number of passengers. The two sets of trains bring back memories of the 1950s, when passenger trains were common throughout the entire iron ore country from the Soo (as the twin cities of Sault Ste. Marie, Ontario and Michigan are known) eastward through Marquette, Escanaba, Iron Mountain, Ironwood, Ashland, Duluth-Superior, and Thunder Bay.

Algoma Central motive power has been repainted in the Wisconsin Central paint schemes. The passenger power, a fleet of FP9s and one FP7, carry an ACR color scheme with Algoma Central lettering to match the streamlined cars of this colorful railroad which serves a part of the world that can only be viewed from a train.

Getting back to the iron ore business, the Algoma Central still plays a minor role in this changing industry. Marquette Range pellets are delivered to the Sault Ste. Marie, Ontario, yard for delivery to Algoma Steel. Although the chapter on the ACR ore business came to an end in 1998, the railroad continues to play a very active and important role in the economy of Northern Ontario.

The ore cars in the photo above were eventually replaced with 100-ton ore cars of two varieties. One was an outside braced car with end platforms (see page 68). The other design was a rounded-side car, such as the 8015 shown here in August 1998. The cars have been transferred to the Wisconsin Central since mining has ceased at Wawa, and now carry WC initials. PATRICK C. DORIN

Algoma Central was noted for its covered turntable at Sault Ste. Marie—a handy thing to have during the snows of winter in Northern Ontario. These ACR units were lined up around the turntable in April 1986. KEVIN J. HOLLAND

The Algoma Central's striking color scheme brightened its north country services including the iron ore traffic to Michipicoten, Ontario (on Lake Superior) and Algoma Steel at Sault Ste. Marie. This ore train, led by GP38-2 No. 2006, was at Michipicoten in February 1995. STEVE GLISCHINSKI

ABOVE: The Soo Line ore dock in Ashland, Wisconsin, served both the Soo Line and the C&NW. This photo shows the *Denmark* loading ore, with the remains of the first Wisconsin Central ore dock visible at right. SOO LINE

FACING PAGE: The former DSS&A line east of the Marquette Range saw a brief resumption of ore train services during the late 1970s. Ore trains were routed over the Soo Line to Sault Ste. Marie for Algoma Steel. This eastbound ore extra is passing the Newberry, Michigan, depot en route to Trout Lake on March 23, 1977. STEVE GLISCHINSKI

The Soo Line Railroad is completely out of the ore business in the State of Michigan—not only that, but the railroad no longer exists in Michigan in any way, shape or form. The Wisconsin Central purchased all of the remaining lines of the former DSS&A and the Soo Line throughout the Upper Peninsula. Let's backtrack a bit, however, and take a look at the operations of the Soo/DSS&A in Michigan and the Canadian Pacific in Ontario.

The Soo Line operated the Duluth, South Shore & Atlantic Railroad ore lines between Marquette and Champion, Michigan, after the companies' 1960 merger. During the last decade of operations between 1960 and 1970, the Soo operated two to four trains per day between Marquette and the Hogan Ore Yard near Negaunee. An

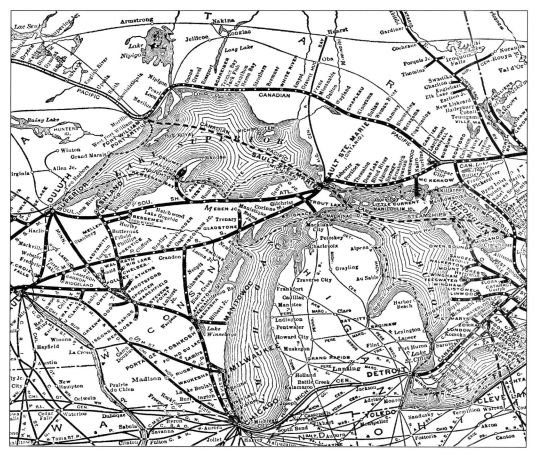

additional train was operated between Marquette and the Champion Mine on almost a daily basis. Consists varied from 30 to 60 cars on the Marquette Range—the shortest trains to be found on any of the ore lines.

THE MARQUETTE RANGE

The DSS&A Baldwins powered the ore trains during the first few years after the Soo Line-South Shore merger, and then were replaced by Soo Line F7s, GP7s, and GP9s.

Ore dock operations were powered by one or two of these Soo Geeps, and sometimes with a Geep and an F7. Ore dock "shoves" ranged from about 25 cars to 35 cars depending upon the motive power, and if the shove originated from the ore yard west of the ore dock.

Interchange ore from the Lake Superior & Ishpeming Railroad had to be pulled up the hill from the main yard east of downtown Marquette and adjacent to Lake Superior. This operation required two locomotives for the ore dock switch assignment. The crew would pull the LS&I ore cars up the hill and into the ore yard. At the ore yard, they would reverse their movement and begin the shove onto the ore dock itself.

The DSS&A ore dock was 900 feet long, and for a while was the third shortest ore dock on the Great Lakes. (CN's dock in Port Arthur was once 600 feet long, and the DM&IR's No. 6 dock in Two Harbors was 888 feet long.) The former DSS&A dock had been scheduled for dismantling several times, and it was finally removed in 2000. The South Shore's dock was the second-last pocket-type ore dock ever built, with construction taking place in 1931. It had a 40-year history of operation.

The Soo Line's Marquette Range operations handled only natural iron ores, but did interchange pellets with the LS&I in Marquette. In some cases, the pellets were mixed with various iron ores on the South Shore ore dock.

The Soo Line's history came to an end in Michigan's Upper Peninsula when the Wisconsin Central took over the operation of all the former Soo and DSS&A routes in 1987.

THE GOGEBIC RANGE

There has not been any mining in the former Soo Line territory between Wakefield, Michigan, and Park Falls, Wisconsin, since 1965. There were, however, two rather interesting traffic

The South Shore's Baldwin road switcher, No. 205, is bringing interchange ore from the LS&I into the ore yard in Marquette on August 23, 1961. The LS&I delivered the ore to the DSS&A's main freight yard along the lakefront. The ore would later be dumped on the ore dock for mixing with ores from mines served by the DSS&A according to steel company specifications. ROBERT C. ANDERSON

DSS&A RS-1 No. 104 has the Pullman-coach-combine *Superior* and Budd RDC-1 No. 500 in tow at Shingleton, Michigan, on August 7, 1956. The "Shoreliner" RDC had broken down and was being towed empty to Marquette for repairs. TLC PUBLISHING COLLECTION

DSS&A No. 303 switching at Newberry, Michigan, on July 23, 1956. The Baldwin-Lima-Westinghouse centercab was built in August 1950.

Sister unit No. 301 passed through Newberry pulling a westbound wayfreight from St. Ignace to Marquette on July 18, 1956.

On June 24, 1956, DSS&A RS-1 No. 104 idled at St. Ignace, Michigan, with the carferry *Chief Wawatam* in the background. ALL, TLC PUBLISHING COLLECTION

DSS&A RS-1 No. 103 was photographed at the Sault Ste. Marie, Michigan, engine terminal on June 24, 1956.

This trio of DSS&A ore cars—Nos. 9574, 9583, and 9563—was loaded with gravel at Newberry, Michigan, on July 18, 1956.

DSS&A "Merchandise Service" double-sheathed, steel-end box car No. 18028 was spotted at Newberry, Michigan, on June 25, 1956. Car was painted a deep yellow, with red and white lettering. ALL, TLC PUBLISHING COLLECTION

A pair of cabooses—DSS&A No. 592 and Soo Line No. 147— waited near the Sault Ste. Marie, Michigan, roundhouse for their next call to duty on June 24, 1956.

DSS&A caboose No. 578 carried the markers of a freight train just east of Marquette on July 6, 1956. BOTH, TLC PUBLISHING COLLECTION

movements of iron ore. The former Bessemer Branch was purchased by the Wisconsin & Michigan Railroad. The W&M moved a few carloads of iron ore from the old Peterson Mine during the early 1990s for a paint producer. These carloads were interchanged with the Wisconsin Central at Mellen, Wisconsin.

The W&M folded rather quickly and the line has been dismantled. The company had run some passenger excursions between Hoyt, Wisconsin, and Bessemer, but there was not enough business to keep the line afloat.

The other ore movement involved the trucking of some of the Peterson Mine ore to the former DSS&A line by North Ironwood, Michigan, for the same paint manufacturer.

Note the offices extending over the side of the Soo Line's Ashland ore dock in this view from the late 1950s. Soo Line

The former DSS&A ore dock at Marquette was still intact in August 1998 but was dismantled in 2000. Patrick C. Dorin

One of the ore trains routed over the Soo (former DSS&A) to Algoma Steel in Sault Ste. Marie, Ontario, LS&I 2300 East is passing the Seney, Michigan depot on March 23, 1977. Some all-rail ore trains also operated over this route to Chicago, ie., from the Marquette area to Trout Lake, and then turning west back to Gladstone and Pembine before heading south toward Chicago. STEVE GLISCHINSKI

This tug is dwarfed by the concrete structure of the former Duluth, South Shore & Atlantic Railroad ore dock at Marquette, Michigan.

The South Shore ore dock approach went through the downtown business district of Marquette. One of the bridges proudly advertised "Marquette—Home of Northern Michigan University."
BOTH, PATRICK C. DORIN

As of 2002, there had not been any other mining activity on the Gogebic or the Penokee Ranges between Wakefield and Park Falls.

The Soo Line history of ore operations in the Upper Peninsula is now folded into the Wisconsin Central, which handles copper products for the smelter at the White Pine Mine location north of Bergland, Michigan.

A SHORT NOTE ON SOO LINE ORE CARS

The Soo Line completed its Marquette ore operations with the 50-ton capacity ore cars that had been in service since the 1920s and even earlier. Soo Line ore cars later went into rock and ballast service, and were scrapped over a period of years. None of the Soo Line cars received any side extensions for pellet service. All of the cars were

off the roster by the late 1980s, prior to the inclusion of the Soo Line into the Canadian Pacific Railway System.

THE CANADIAN PACIFIC RAILWAY

The Canadian Pacific Railway was also an ore hauler for Great Lakes shipping. The CPR's operation was a bit different from those of the other ore haulers in the Lake Superior and Lake-Huron region.

The CPR served an iron recovery mill at the International Nickel Company's (Inco) Copper Cliff Smelter, which was 80 miles from the Lake Huron railhead at Little Current, Ontario. Iron is a by-product of processing nickel-iron-copper-sulphide ores.

The CPR transported the ore product in a group of cars, some of which were ordered as early as 1925 from the Canadian Car & Foundry Company (CC&F). These cars were numbered from 376500 to 376846. One hundred of the cars were rebuilt with 18-inch side extensions. The cars were 31 feet, 2-5/8 inches long inside the coupler faces with a height of 9 feet, 4-1/8 inches prior to the addition of the side extensions.

The cars' capacity was originally 75 tons, but with rebuilding the cars were reclassified to carry 81 tons. The gondola-type CPR ore cars were equipped with five drop-bottom doors on each side.

The Canadian Pacific ore dock at Little Current was equipped with a bridge with a seven-ton clam for about a 500-ton loading rate. The dock was 1500 feet long with a 50,000-ton capacity. Construction took place around 1915.

Before completing this section, it should be mentioned that the Canadian Pacific operated a fleet of ore cars that were similar to the Lake Superior cars. Numbered 377000 to 377249, the cars were 27 feet, 2 inches over the strikers as compared to 21 feet, 6 inches (plus or minus) for the Lake Superior ore cars.

A FINAL NOTE

The Soo Line's iron ore routes extended from the Ironwood-Bessemer Area on the Gogebic Range to Ashland via Mellen. The DSS&A/Soo Line routes extended from west of Ishpeming and Humboldt to Marquette.

The CPR route extended from Copper Cliff, Ontario—just east of Sudbury—to Little Current on Manitoulin Island in Lake Huron.

Canadian Pacific 376554 (from series 376500-376846), at Brandon, Manitoba, in October 1987 was once part of the fleet providing ore service between Copper Cliff and Little Current. FRED HEADON

The Canadian Pacific ore cars most resembling the "Lake Superior" ore car design were the rectangular-side cars, CPR series 377000 to 377249. The major differences were the length, as well as the three ribs and the higher cubic capacity. The CPR cars were 11 feet, 9 inches high whereas the Minnesota rectangular-side cars were 10 feet, 2 inches high. This equipment was normally assigned to lead-zinc ore and concentrate service in British Columbia. Four of the cars were tested in Sudbury, Ontario, in 1978. Evidently, the cars were not suited to the commodities handled in the Sudbury nickel industry because the short drop-bottom gondola cars continued to be the preferred car. Lead-zinc ores being lighter than iron ore, a larger volume can be carried within the allowable axle loading, hence the longer and taller car to contain the larger volume. The four cars were Nos. 377060, 377017, 377185, and 377246, shown at Sudbury in October 1978. GORDON D. JOMINI

THE FINAL ORE CAR FLEET FOR MICHIGAN

50-Ton Ore Cars
Duluth, South Shore & Atlantic Railroad—
Marquette Range

Series	Quantity	Remarks
9000 - 9398	374 Cars	Full-side cars with side bracing
9400 - 9524	123 Cars	Sloped-end cars
9525 - 9674	138 Cars	Summers ore cars

Soo Line Railroad—
Marquette and Gogebic Ranges

Series	Quantity	Remarks
25703 - 26699	476 Cars	Sloped-end cars
80002 - 80199	101 Cars	Summers ore cars
80200 - 80507	283 Cars	Rectangular-side cars with side bracing
80508 - 81599	924 Cars	Sloped-end ore cars

THE MILWAUKEE ROAD
THE ESCANABA 8

ABOVE: Although the ore business is long gone, the E&LS had a small fleet of ore cars. No. 3043, photographed in 1998, had extrended sides and has been used for rock service. PATRICK C. DORIN

FACING PAGE: Ore traffic was still going strong in the Upper Peninsula of Michigan in June 1977. This five-unit Milwaukee Road consist includes two Geeps and three F-units, one of which is in the passenger or Union Pacific colors. This is but another example of the diversity to be found on the ore lines. Milwaukee No. 314 is doing the honors near Groveland Junction, north of Iron Mountain. STEVE GLISCHINSKI

The Milwaukee Road began its ore-hauling career in 1887 with a joint operating agreement with the Soo Line. The Milwaukee served the new Memominee Range and interchanged ore traffic with the Soo Line at Pembine. With the completion of the Milwaukee Road ore docks in 1905 at Escanaba, the company withdrew from the Soo Line and operated over the Escanaba & Lake Superior between Channing and Escanaba.

The next chapter of the Milwaukee Road's pool-service operating agreements began during the early part of the Great Depression. The Chicago & North Western also served the Menominee Range, and with the massive declines in ore traffic and revenues, the Milwaukee and C&NW joined forces to provide a new level of service. The

Milwaukee Road was to supply approximately one-third of the rolling stock, motive power, and crews, and would earn the equivalent in revenue. This pooling arrangement continued until the Milwaukee Road sold its rail lines north of Green Bay, Wisconsin, to an expanded Escanaba & Lake Superior Railroad in 1980.

The Milwaukee Road served only the Groveland mine and pellet plant located north of Iron Mountain when the trackage was sold to the E&LS. Sadly, all of the Milwaukee Road ore cars had disappeared from the scene, and only C&NW power and ore cars operated between the Groveland Mine and Iron Mountain.

During the 1960s, 1970s, and 1980s, the Milwaukee Road participated in all-rail ore movements from both the Michigan Ranges and the Mesabi Range.

Michigan ore was often handled in the regularly scheduled time freights through Green Bay and Milwaukee to Chicago for Illinois- and Indiana-area steel mills. Mesabi ore traveled in solid trainloads from Duluth to Chicago for interchange with the Norfolk & Western and forwarding to eastern destinations.

In the diesel era, the Milwaukee Road's ore trains were powered by Fairbanks-Morse motive power, and then by Electro-Motive power ranging from GP9s to GP38-2s and GP40s and the powerful SD40-2. The Milwaukee Road's orange-and-black diesel power seemed to be a natural complement for the boxcar-red ore cars punctuated by an orange bay-window caboose. What a sight!

The Milwaukee Road was out of the ore business by the time of its purchase by the Soo Line in 1985. The Soo Line, today under the Canadian Pacific banner, does not handle any ore traffic over the former Milwaukee Road routings. The Twin Cities–Duluth–Superior route (former Great Northern trackage) does, however, see a substantial amount of all-rail ore traffic on Chicago & North Western (now Union Pacific) and Burlington Northern (now BNSF) trains.

The Milwaukee Road participated in the movement of ore traffic from the Menominee Range with its route from Iron River to Iron Mountain and the C&NW ore pool. The company also handled iron ore from Champion on the Marquette Range.

Prior to the Chicago & North Western ore pooling agreement, the Milwaukee Road sent its ore trains to Channing for their trackage rights over the E&LS between Channing and the company ore docks at Escanaba.

Going one more step back in history, prior to the E&LS trackage rights agreement to Escanaba, Milwaukee Road ore trains operated south to Pembine for movement to a Gladstone ore dock over the Soo Line.

MAIN MAP: The Escanaba & Lake Superior Railroad and its connections. E&LS

INSET: The Milwaukee Road's ore lines in Wisconsin and Michigan. MILWAUKEE ROAD

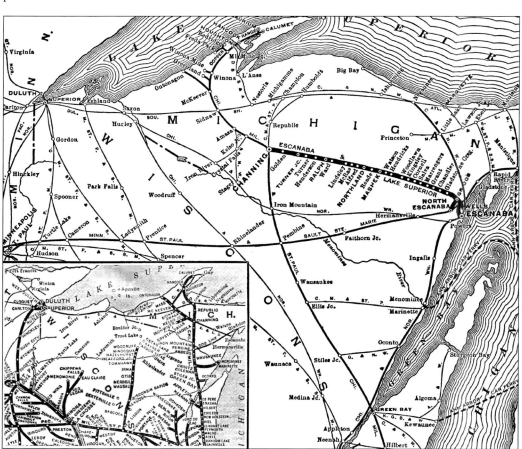

The final E&LS ore movements, in 1980-82, took place between the Groveland Mine and the interchange with the C&NW at Iron Mountain.

All-rail ore movements operated south out of Iron Mountain for the Michigan Ranges. Interchange all-rail ore from Minnesota was handled south out of Duluth over the former Northern Pacific and Burlington Northern

THE ORE CAR FLEET

Depending upon steel mill destinations, the Milwaukee Road ore trains consisted of rebuilt ribside hopper cars or DM&IR ore cars. The Milwaukee cars operated in both Mesabi and Michigan trains, while the DM&IR cars were used almost exclusively from the Minntac plant

Ore car No. 75203, at Eau Claire, Wisconsin, in 1955 illustrates the second phase of lettering for the Milwaukee Road fleet. The car is virtually identical to the Model Die Casting rectangular-side HO-scale ore cars. J. M. GRUBER COLLECTION

Milwaukee Road ore car No. 76689 carries the most prominent of the final ore car paint and lettering schemes. It is shown at Iron Mountain in 1972. When the railroad rebuilt part of its fleet with 18-inch side extensions, the cars were renumbered 76650-76999. They were also equipped with clamp brackets for the new rotary dumping facility at the Escanaba dock. PATRICK C. DORIN

The Milwaukee Road's 1600-hp Fairbanks-Morse road switchers played an important role in the Milwaukee Road-C&NW ore pool. No. 548 is switching ore cars at the Escanaba ore yard in July 1966.
Owen Leander,
J. Michael Gruber Collection

A Milwaukee Road Fairbanks-Morse road switcher is shoving a cut of loaded ore cars onto the C&NW No. 6 ore dock at Escanaba in September 1965. The wooden ore dock had only about three more years of operation before being replaced by the new low-level dock.
Patrick C. Dorin

near Mountain Iron, Minnesota.

Modelers should note that the Milwaukee Road ore car is the prototype for Model Die Casting's rectangular-side HO-scale ore car. The Walthers lettering arrangement for their special-run Milwaukee Road scheme was correct for the final years of this rather special 70-ton-capacity ore car. The Model Die Casting factory lettering is correct for the 1930s and 1940s periods.

The Milwaukee Road ore cars were mixed with C&NW cars, as well as with the LS&I ore cars. A modeler could easily, and correctly, assemble a train consisting of ore cars from all three railroads. Furthermore, Milwaukee Road

ore cars could be found on a regular basis in Soo Line trains on the old Gladstone (Michigan) Division during the 1950s and perhaps even into the 1960s. Finally, Milwaukee Road ore cars could be found mixed with Northern Pacific ore cars when used for ballast service on the ex-NP line between Duluth and St. Paul.

Milwaukee Road ore cars went south to Indiana for coal service during the winter season. Indeed a major percentage of the fleet was lettered for Milwaukee subsidiary Chicago, Terra Haute & Southeastern Railroad. Such operations added new levels of variety to the iron ore railroading of the Milwaukee Road.

The Milwaukee Road played an important role in all-rail ore services for many years. In this trio of photos, the Milwaukee Road is delivering an all-rail empty train to the Duluth, Missabe & Iron Range in June 1980, with a consist of DM&IR ore cars. Milwaukee Road 183 West is rolling over the Burlington Northern toward Duluth, Minnesota. The train is just south of North Branch, Minnesota. A rib-sided, bay window caboose brings up the rear of the 105-car train.
ALL, PATRICK C. DORIN

Three Milwaukee Road F-units led by FP7A No. 63A head up an ore train at Antoine, Michigan, on October 28, 1978. The yard is near Iron Mountain, where the Milwaukee Road and Chicago & North Western exchanged empty and loaded ore trains for the Groveland Mine during the last few years of the Menominee Range ore pool. STEVE GLISCHINSKI

This is indeed a rare photograph of a Groveland Mine run with a solitary F7, No. 108A, and a block of Lake Superior & Ishpeming Railroad ore cars on March 22, 1979. While the car count of this loaded train was not recorded, a reasonable estimate would be from 30 to 50 cars behind a single 1500-hp locomotive. During the final years of the ore pool, it was not uncommon to see LS&I ore cars mixed with C&NW cars. STEVE GLISCHINSKI

THE ESCANABA & LAKE SUPERIOR RAILROAD

The E&LS has had two periods of iron ore traffic history, and both involved the Milwaukee Road in two different ways.

The Escanaba & Lake Superior's first "iron ore" era involved Milwaukee Road trackage rights from Channing to Escanaba. This began in 1901 when the Milwaukee Road completed the construction of their own ore docks in Escanaba. The Milwaukee Road had worked out a trackage rights agreement with the E&LS, and Milwaukee Road steam power handled the trains to and from the Lake Michigan port. The Milwaukee Road ore operations continued over the E&LS through the iron ore shipping season of 1934. A new ore pooling agreement with the C&NW brought an end to ore trains on the E&LS for over three decades.

The next era began in 1980 when the Milwaukee Road sold their trackage from Green Bay to northern Michigan to the E&LS. At that time, the Milwaukee Road was still serving the Groveland Mine and pelletizing plant north of Iron Mountain near Randville. This operation

was part of the ore pooling agreement with the C&NW, which delivered the empty trains to the Milwaukee at Antoine. The empties were then delivered to the mine, the loads picked up, and brought back to Antoine and C&NW trackage. The E&LS continued this operation but not as part of the original Milwaukee Road-C&NW ore pooling agreement. The new operation was basically an interchange operation with the E&LS crews handling the ore trains to and from the Groveland facilities. E&LS ore operations ceased in 1982 when the Groveland Mine was closed.

The E&LS handled slightly less than two million tons of pellets per year while they participated in this operation. The ore trains shared the E&LS main line with the regular freight between Green Bay, Iron Mountain, and Ontonagon. Generally, the E&LS operated at least one loaded and empty train movement per day, but sometimes there could be two such trains in each direction.

The E&LS did not own any ore cars for this operation. In fact, the Milwaukee Road ore cars did not survive or stay in the area. The final train

Twin hopper No. 95612 is an example of the coal hoppers rebuilt with larger cubic capacities for all-rail ore service from both the Mesabi and Menominee Ranges. PATRICK C. DORIN

Groveland Junction, Michigan, is the point where the E&LS and Milwaukee Road trains left the main line for the Groveland Mine. Conrail power visited on May 26, 1983. STEVE GLISCHINSKI

An Escanaba & Lake Superior Baldwin road switcher—in its Great Northern-inspired colors—leads a Conrail unit at Iron Mountain, Michigan, on May 26, 1983. STEVE GLISCHINSKI

The same day, at Merriman, Michigan, the Conrail unit is leading the empty mine run. Who would have expected to find Conrail motive power handling ore in Upper Michigan? STEVE GLISCHINSKI

By 1980, the Escanaba & Lake Superior had taken over the Milwaukee Road trackage and was handling the ore trains between the C&NW and the Groveland Mine. On August 3, 1980, two Conrail units were moving the empty train to the mine through Groveland Junction. The consist included C&NW ore cars, with a mixture of LS&I ore cars replacing some Milwaukee Road equipment. The Milwaukee Road's final curtain has been dropped.
STEVE GLISCHINSKI

On May 23, 1980, at Iron Mountain, Michigan, this E&LS ore train from the C&NW was powered by leased Conrail EMD's—quite a different look from the days of yellow-and-green C&NW power and orange-and-black on the Milwaukee Road.
STEVE GLISCHINSKI

operations consisted solely of C&NW ore cars. One could, however, find Lake Superior & Ishpeming Railroad cars mixed in the trains to and from the C&NW.

The E&LS did own a very small number of ore cars for rock service.

The future of ore operations on the E&LS is not promising at this writing. The company handles a substantial amount of pulpwood and paper products, and is the economic lifeline for many Upper Michigan communities. Without the E&LS, future industrialization and expansion would not be possible, and that, of course, includes mining operations.

This May 23, 1980, ore train at Iron Mountain included an E&LS caboose. STEVE GLISCHINSKI

The Groveland Mine was the last mine to operate on the Menominee Range. The Escanaba & Lake Superior carried out a rather interesting train operation with its exotic mixture of motive power, as here on May 26, 1983. STEVE GLISCHINSKI

MILWAUKEE ROAD ORE CAR ROSTER

Late 1960s to early 1970s

75001 - 76599
Odd numbers; 444 cars without extensions

76650 - 76999
Odd and even numbers;
350 cars with 18-inch extensions

The Milwaukee Road owned and operated
182 cars without extensions, with only eight
cars remaining with extensions by 1976.

SELECTED ANNUAL ORE TONNAGES FOR THE MILWAUKEE ROAD

Menominee Range

1953	1,584,019 tons
1957	1,460,500 tons
1962	1,131,842 tons
1965	1,491,145 tons
1970	974,691 tons
1971	1,070,795 tons
1973	773,982 tons
1975	750,098 tons
1976	584,812 tons
1977	803,058 tons

7 CANADIAN NATIONAL

ABOVE: Numerous CN ore cars were stored at Depot Harbour, Ontario, for a time after the Moose Mountain ore traffic ended. This view is looking eastward toward South Parry. The main spur track is to the left. GORDON D. JOMINI

FACING PAGE: On May 25, 1973, CN SD40s Nos. 5078 and 5022 led an eastbound empty train back to the mainland en route to Moose Mountain from Parry Island after dumping iron ore at the Depot Harbour dock. ELMER TRELOAR, PATRICK C. DORIN COLLECTION

The Canadian National Railway tops off this book on the Michigan ore lines, or by stretching it a bit—the ore lines east on the CNR. Although the services were not as large as the lines west, there were a number of interesting variations.

National Steel Company developed a mine and pelletizing plant at Moose Mountain, north of Sudbury, Ontario, in 1959. The iron ore pellets were transported from Moose Mountain by the CNR over its Bala Subdivision to South Parry, and then over the 7.6-mile Depot Harbour spur. Upon arrival at the Georgian Bay ore dock, crews spotted the loads at the dumper and shoved the cars through as they were unloaded. Conveyor belts handled the pellets to the stockpiles and later to the boats. The dock had a 300,000-ton storage capacity and was

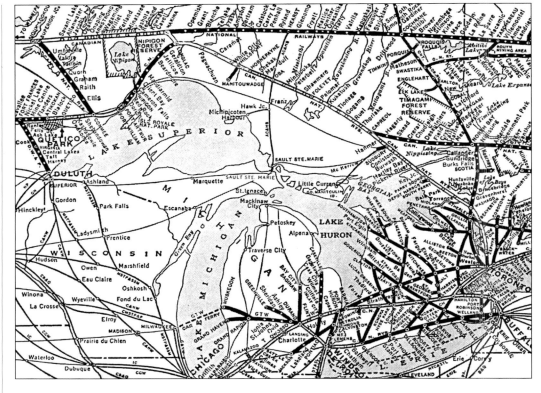

800 feet long. This operation ended in 1990.

While the Moose Mountain operation was a traditional rail-to-lake shipment, the Sherman Mine at Temagami, Ontario, on the Ontario Northland Railway was an all-rail routing. The CN interchanged the ore traffic at North Bay, Ontario. In this case, the pellets were handled in covered ore cars for movement to the steel mills at Hamilton, Ontario.

Still another ONR-CNR operation involved all-rail shipments from the Adams Mine to steel plants in Ohio. This ore was handled in 70- and 100-ton-capacity open-top hopper cars.

The ore traffic was a colorful chapter in the history of freight services. However, all of the ore deposits in Ontario have not been exhausted. One can dream of future ore operations, and such just might be the case. Will it be in the 24-foot ore cars? Probably not, but one can be sure the new operations will be no less exciting.

On April 7, 1971, GP9s Nos. 4573 and 4581 handle an eastbound empty ore train from Depot Harbour, Ontario, three miles south of Parry Sound. The train consisted of the CN's 82-1/2-ton ore cars with side extensions. ELMER TRELOAR, PATRICK C. DORIN COLLECTION

Canadian National is back in the ore business. With CN's purchase of the Wisconsin Central came the WC's Michigan ore lines and the Minorca trains between the DM&IR connection at Steelton (Duluth) to Escanaba. This ore empty has just arrived at the Steelton Yard from CN's Wisconsin Central Division. Two Illinois Central SD40-2s head a train of rebuilt SSAM ore cars. PATRICK C. DORIN